SHERMAN, RICHARD
#19, #5
$1.25

RICHARD SHERMAN
702 EAST VISTA WAY
VISTA, CALIF.
PHONE PALACE 4-4110

$1.25

70¢

RICHARD SHERMAN
702 EAST VISTA WAY
VISTA, CALIF.
PHONE PALACE 4-4110

FRIENDS AND ENEMIES

BOOKS BY ADLAI E. STEVENSON

MAJOR CAMPAIGN SPEECHES

CALL TO GREATNESS

WHAT I THINK

THE NEW AMERICA

FRIENDS AND ENEMIES

FRIENDS AND ENEMIES

What I Learned in Russia

ADLAI E. STEVENSON

New York
HARPER & BROTHERS PUBLISHERS

Library of Congress catalog card number: 59-8246

For my traveling companions to Siberia—and back!—

Bob Tucker and Bill Blair,

Borden and John Fell Stevenson

Contents

*Sixteen pages of photographs
will be found following page 38*

PUBLISHER'S NOTE

Harper & Brothers is proud to publish this collection of Adlai Stevenson's reports of his unusual visit to the Soviet Union in the summer of 1958. These penetrating and readable articles attracted widespread attention all over the world at the time of their serial publication.

This book is in response to many requests for their publication in collected form. We have edited Governor Stevenson's articles very slightly, not for substance but for book publication.

Introduction

THIS is not a "book" about Russia; it is a collection of brief reports about a journey through the Soviet Union during the summer of 1958. They were written and published serially after my return in the autumn and have not been revised in substance. My sons Borden and John Fell, who were with me, took the photographs.

In 1926, as a young man, I traveled across the young Soviet Union from the Caucasus to Finland. This time, thirty-two years later, I traveled from Finland out to Central Asia and Siberia—including areas closed to foreigners which the Soviet Government kindly opened to me.

Like all Americans I am curious about Russia, which has contradicted our ideas, organized a vast empire, raised our taxes, and challenged the United States to political, economic and military competition everywhere—all in forty years. That is why I went back—to see the Russia of today and its leaders for myself. What I saw and heard I attempted to summarize in these reports when I came home. They suffer from all the frailties of first impression, abbreviation and my limited perception.

The changes I saw in the Soviet Union after thirty years did not surprise me very much—except that the people were more friendly, their ignorance and anxiety about America greater, and the industrialization more spectacular than I had expected.

The journey confirmed my impression that no relaxation in the Communist offensive is imminent and that there are no visible signs of internal weakness or upheaval in the Soviet Union. On the contrary, the material achievements are profoundly impressive; the vast Russian land is beginning to yield up its wealth; and most Soviet citizens are proud and loyal, like most citizens everywhere. Nor could I detect that our negative policy toward the Soviet Union was likely to induce the Soviet collapse which has been periodically foretold from official Washington in recent years, or even contain the expansion of Soviet influence.

But the Communist system *has* frailties. The imperial Czars' successors were chosen by dynastic inheritance, but in the Soviet autocracy no system of orderly transfer of power without conspiracy, violence and exile has been evolved. The present massive stability of the U.S.S.R. obscures the insidious instability of a big, modern, industrial state ruled autocratically. When a system, like the Soviet, lacks a legalized opposition, it is inherently unstable. And I suspect the reason they have not solved the problem of orderly transfer of power is that it is insoluble in the dictatorial framework.

The Russian people have never known real democracy. They passed by revolution from Czarism to Soviet Communism with only moments of chaotic liberalism. But

Russia has a long tradition, especially among the intelligentsia, of aspiration for individual freedom, and for the whole scale of humane and compassionate values. It is a tradition so profound that no surface revolution can erase it. The very violence of the recent official outcry against Boris Pasternak, who has voiced in print the claims of the human spirit, testifies to the fear of its revival. And—who knows?—perhaps the drama of the lonely Pasternak is one of those "portents of freedom" in Russia of which he writes. And we can find some sober, long-range hope in history's lesson that dictatorship is never eternal.

But I came away from this vibrant country with a much clearer feeling for the people's hunger for peace and dread of another war. I felt that the Russian people are really more fearful of the United States than we are of them, which is not hard to understand in view of our ring of air bases and the incessant propaganda about the hostility of the "ruling cliques of the imperialist-capitalist powers." Assuming we do not invite Soviet military adventure by our weakness, I do not fear a third world war. They know the terrible consequences; the very words "world war" themselves are obsolete as a description of national suicide. But to avoid mutual suicide we are both piling up weapons to shoot at one another. It doesn't make sense, especially to the poor and fearful bystanders—a fact the Soviet peace propaganda skillfully exploits.

Moreover, large-scale war would interrupt the huge economic development program which has been rapidly transforming this backward agrarian system into a highly industrialized, modern state—by methods and at a price, to be sure, which no democratic people would long tolerate. The United States and "the capitalists" are still the deadly demons of Soviet propaganda. And one is amused by the spectacle of a whole nation damning "capitalists" and the United States, while at the same time busily trying to "catch up" with the United States and the hated capitalists. The new seven-year plan for industrial development, if achieved, will bring Russia close to American living standards in another decade. War could only further postpone the day when the long-suffering, hard-working Russian people begin to enjoy the fruits of their toil and relief from the grinding austerity of the past.

On the assumption that well-to-do people are more passive and peaceful than the envious and poor, the liberalizing tendencies in Russia should increase as prosperity increases. So why not trade with them? Why not help them improve living standards? Why not encourage the growth of material abundance and thereby make it harder to preserve the secrecy, ignorance and tight controls of the Soviet system? Why not help the Soviet leaders subvert their own system of fear with the confidence bred of plenty? And especially why not—when our refusal to trade with them has not stopped them from developing the Soviet economy at a spectacular pace?

The Soviet leaders attach topmost priority to the success of their new seven-year development plan. The goals are so ambitious, however, that there must be grave doubt whether they can be reached without reducing military expenditures. And the strain will increase in 1960 when the Russian manpower shortage, resulting from the German invasion in the last war, will become most severe. The foreseeable conflicting demands of heavy industry, consumer goods and military spending suggest that we may be fast approaching the time when the Russians may be more receptive to détente and to serious disarmament proposals—an opportunity we should not overlook. Already the Russians are asking quiet questions about the effect of reduced military spending on the *American* economy.

But there is risk as well as hope in Russia's economic forward surge. The relaxing, liberalizing effect of prosperity and equality which we can hope for is not as evident as Soviet scientific progress and military might. Probably a fourth of Russia's production goes into the war potential, and in the new seven-year plan the military program still seems to get first priority. Then follows the development of China and the Communist bloc; the ambitious economic offensive using trade and aid as the major weapon of Soviet foreign policy; and finally, the need to raise living standards.

Dominated by the pragmatic Communism of Nikita Khrushchev's school of thought, the Soviet Union is seeking to insure its military power and security—and it is doing it; it is seeking to develop its limitless resources—and it is doing it; it is seeking to spread its influence far and wide in a world where chaos and misery abound, where new nations are beset with economic difficulties, and where Western democracy is in many places, alas, now on the retreat. And it is doing that too!

The Russians' primary weapon is economic power. They say so themselves. And we should take them seriously. Congress generously supports our defense effort, but every year we have to fight the battle of trade and aid, as if the Russian economic offensive was something temporary and less dangerous or permanent than the military threat. Nor has the Western Alliance faced the realities of the greatest threat of all and concerted its enormous economic power in a coherent counter-offensive.

Evidently the reality of our peril is the most difficult thing for us to accept. Just as I wish Mr. Khrushchev and thousands of Russians of all stations could come here and see what this peaceful, contented, free country is really like, so I wish countless Americans could go where I've gone around the world, see what I've seen, hear what I've heard.

They would see and hear, among other unpleasant things, that the rich nations are getting richer while the poor are getting poorer. This is a disaster for us, the rich, which the Russians are making the most of on a world scale. As a poor nation that has pulled itself up by its own bootstraps, as it were, Russia has a great attraction to other poor nations who are natively suspicious of the West, or have been disaffected by our military bargaining and self-righteous moralizing. They would also discover that the Russians conduct their economic offensive in these decisive population areas with many techniques: they sell Russian products at cut prices to get foreign exchange and capture markets; they barter oil and machinery, for example, for South American coffee and wool; they buy commodities other countries desperately want to sell; they loan money at low interest rates, build industrial plants, and provide technicians who speak the languages and live humbly like the local people.

I think our inquiring travelers would come to the conclusion that Soviet economic-political penetration is formidable and succeeding. The extension of Communist control ultimately means strangulation or conformity for us. And it presents some questions that we Americans and our free friends must grapple with.

Can we, will we, take the bold and costly measures to avert disaster in this contest? Can we, will we, make the greater effort—now while there is still time—to arrest the fatal economic deterioration and provide an alternative to Communism as a technique of change and growth in the poor, underdeveloped lands?

But these questions lead to others that we can't avoid much longer.

In the first place, the political-economic contest with the Communist bloc is not a passing nuisance; it will last a long time; it is serious; and it is probably decisive. We in the West will have to learn to conduct it with the same sense of continuity and urgency as we apply to maintaining our military defenses.

It is a fair question whether we can compete with the Soviet state trading system with our free system of private foreign trade. To match their flexibility—their ability to buy, sell and invest where, when and how they please for political advantage—maybe we, too, will have to adopt new methods of state trading, and even combine with other free countries.

And I have saved the hardest questions for the last:

Can our American system prevail in competition with the central planning, control and direction of the Soviet system?

Can we mobilize, organize and utilize our human and natural resources as effectively as they can?

Can we do so without imposing controls that imperil the very freedom and values we in the United States are trying to preserve?

Are our institutions adequate to conduct foreign policy in competition with the speed, secrecy and certainty of the Kremlin?

In a shooting war our system seems to perform more effectively than a dictatorship—or, at least, so the evidence of World Wars I and II suggests. Then everything was subordinated to the demands of victory, and the government was able to make drastic and uncomfortable decisions, promptly and without fear of serious public protest. But in our present situation, the government can rarely act promptly and decisively; often it cannot act at all, because domestic political considerations are *not* subordinated to the needs of an effective foreign policy.

For our Constitution and the unwritten rules of our political system were both designed for a different purpose. They were evolved at a time when we were committed to a policy of nonentanglement with foreign countries. So our Founding Fathers created a system that has proved extremely effective for composing internal differences, but it was not designed for coping with international problems. At the time this weakness did not matter since the oceans provided wonderfully effective protection against all possible enemies.

Now the world is completely different, but our machinery remains the same. Congressmen are bound to be concerned primarily with the demands of their constituents; the national interest is apt to be a secondary consideration. In addition, under our system, any foreign policy measure can be held up or killed by any sizable group in Congress.

Our wheat growers can strain our traditional relations with Canada; the textile interests can cause trouble with Japan and England; Zionists can complicate our relations in the Middle East. And a single Congressman in a strategic position can mess up our immigration laws or cripple our overseas propaganda operations.

In particular, it is immensely difficult for the executive agencies to plan and carry out a coherent, far-sighted strategy of economic warfare, so long as imports, exports and overseas investments are subject to the whims and self-interest of every domestic pressure group. And, as I have said, it is likely that the economic battlefield will prove the decisive one.

Our traditions place us at a disadvantage in several other ways. For example, our habit of making appropriations on an annual basis only. How can India—or a dozen other countries to which American aid is crucial—make long-range economic plans, when they may have to be changed or discarded at the next session of Congress? Or, for that matter, how can *we* plan a long-range, world-wide economic development program with our allies, or a defense program employing missiles and electronic systems which take decades to develop, on the basis of annual appropriations?

Again, how can we develop a foreign service that will attract our ablest talent so long as no pressure group of any consequence has any interest in supporting it? The Russians can order their ablest men into diplomacy or on a disagreeable overseas assignment. But the State Department has to compete against the far higher pay of, say, the advertising and television industries—and no Congressman can hope to win a single vote by fighting to get better pay and representation allowances for the men who are now, literally, the first line of our defense.

What troubles me even more is that the American people are not showing many signs that they are willing to do what is necessary to win the long contest with Russia. They are frittering away talent, time and resources on trivialities—ranging from quiz shows to Detroit's chromium creations—while the Russians are concentrating

everything on their overriding goal. Again, this is partly
due to lack of leadership; Americans have never been told,
by the only men who can command continual national
attention, what has to be done, and what sacrifices they
must make to achieve it. (And if they are told in a political campaign there is, I think, some evidence at least
that they don't like it!)

But I am not sure whether any President can persuade
the country—without the stimulus of war—to do these
things. Maybe our kind of democracy has a fatal addiction
to short views rather than long; to present comforts rather
than future safety; to private satisfactions rather than
public necessities. Else why do we spend more money
on advertising than on college education—on tobacco
than on textbooks—on entertainment than on urban re-
newal?

The next ten years, I would guess, will *really* prove
whether this nation or any nation so conceived and so
dedicated can long endure—and right now the prognosis
is not good. We are losing ground nearly everywhere; we
are not taking measures necessary to stop the loss; and
hardly anybody seems to care. In our complacent, happy
fashion, we assume that we can't lose—that if we stand
firm, persevere and damn the Communists enough, Right
will surely prevail in the end. Well, it didn't once before,
when Athenian democracy was involved in a similar long,
tiresome struggle with Spartan tyranny. On that occasion,
an infinitely superior civilization went under, because
it lacked the self-discipline to survive. One could cite

other examples. Is it happening again, right here and right now?

My conclusion is that our Russian competitors are much tougher than most of us have yet realized—and that this time we might get licked, unless we are willing to change our habits, our political behavior and our complacent outlook on the world.

But the sky to me is not dark. I like to think of the great forward thrust of Communism not as a threat but as a great chance to demonstrate again that only free institutions can achieve the right ends by the right methods and thereby satisfy man's innermost urgings. As Julian Huxley has said: "In lower organisms the only ultimate criterion is survival; but in man some experiences and actions, some objects and ideas, are valued for their own sake."

I confess that whenever I hear talk about what we, the great, free Western democracies—we who value actions and ideas for their own sake—can and cannot do or afford to do, I am reminded of the imperial Manchus who disdained the Western barbarians for inventing steamships. The Manchus were obsolete and their glory and power have vanished long since.

Are we obsolete too? Of course not. Our free economy has just survived the third recession since the war, and again confounded Communism's confident prediction of an inevitable and shattering capitalist depression. Western economic strength has never been greater. And it has expanded and multiplied production and human well-being largely by private investment.

Thus have the free institutions of the West disproved the Socialist doctrine that only government investment and ownership can insure economic growth. One by one the Socialist parties of Europe have abandoned the only basic idea they shared with Communism—government ownership of the means of production. And, one by one, the Communist parties of Europe have lost strength.

We have the supreme advantage of living under the economic and political system that most people want, as history teaches us. Once we are fully aware that the system is in danger I have no doubt what we will do. And that's why these reports on Russia end on a note of "calm and final confidence."

ADLAI E. STEVENSON

Libertyville, Illinois
January 10, 1959

FRIENDS AND ENEMIES

CHAPTER I

Talking with Khrushchev

"MEN WORKING" is the symbol of Russia today as I saw it over some 7,000 miles, from the Gulf of Finland through Siberia to Central Asia and the Chinese border.

I visited huge farms and factories, government officials and scientific centers, schools and universities, power stations and housing projects, and talked with people in many different walks of life. The image I brought back with me was of a vast, rich, underdeveloped country hard at work with single-minded purpose to build itself up to challenge America's world leadership. The whole gigantic power apparatus—education, science, industry, agriculture and administration—is harnessed with ruthless, concentrated purpose on increased production, higher living standards, security, power and influence. Overtake, catch up, compete—beat the U.S.! This is the constant refrain of signs, songs, speeches and the monotonous heavy-handed propaganda which is omnipresent in Soviet life.

Even the Minister of Education, after remarking that we teach home economics to schoolgirls better than they do, quickly added, "But we are going to catch up with you!" From Leningrad to Tashkent, from Minsk to Novosibirsk, posters proclaim this ambition in pithy phrases, and exhort the workers to greater efforts.

Here and there you see billboards saying "Use air transport," or "Drink Soviet champagne," or "Put your money in savings banks." And, by the way, there is no place else to put it, if you have any, except in government bonds paying the same rate of interest—3 per cent.

But the political propaganda is more interesting. "The People and the Party are One!" or "Communism is the Bright Tomorrow of All Mankind," reads the worker on the wall of his factory. "Thanks to the Party and the Government for Our Happy Childhood," read the children at the entrance to the House of the Young Pioneers. "The U.S.S.R. is a Great Railroad Power," says the sign on a trestle. "Glory to the Communist Party of the Soviet Union!" is the legend on huge red banners in the great stadiums.

Catch up with America; Save the Peace; Build Communism; Work! Work! Work!—all combine to replace individual thinking with automatic mass reflexes. And all combine to convey to the visitor a sense of unremitting pressure. I suspect that many Russians become inured to it and develop a sales resistance. And it seemed to me that people must crave respite from the incessant exhortation.

But in one respect they don't need to catch up with anybody—hospitality! It is exhilarating, exhausting and evidently impervious to propaganda. While I and my companions were traveling through the U.S.S.R., the American Embassy in Moscow was attacked by a mob and the press, radio and party were screaming the "people's wrath" about American "aggression" in the Middle East day and night. But the same "people" greeted us everywhere with eager, friendly, even moving enthusiasm. In personal contact, even their leaders were friendly and hospitable.

The day following Nikita Khrushchev's secret trip to Peiping, I had just finished an immense and good-humored lunch with the acting Foreign Minister and some of his colleagues in a great prerevolutionary house when they suddenly informed me that I was to visit the Premier in a few minutes. My object was a brief call to thank him for the extraordinary hospitality I had enjoyed everywhere, in city and village, office and factory.

Mr. Khrushchev received me for what turned out to be a wide-ranging two-and-one-half-hour conversation in his long, narrow, plain office in the old Royal Palace of the Kremlin. Portraits of Marx and Lenin looked down from the dun-colored walls (in the provinces, Stalin is still looking down, too). Mr. Khrushchev is a short, stout, bald man who looks his age of sixty-four. His manner is unpretentious and jovial; his laugh is quick and infectious, and there is an unmistakable ring of authority in his low voice. He looked tired and lacked the bounce I had expected.

But this may have been a result of his unheralded four-day visit to Peiping, where he had conferred with Mao Tse-tung and the Chinese Communist leaders. And, as we talked, I felt reinforced in the conclusion based on previous talks with many European leaders and other Soviet officials—that Communist China bulks very large in Soviet thought, concern and policy today.

Anticipating the substance of a letter to President Eisenhower which was to be released six hours later, Mr. Khrushchev brusquely rejected the idea, which he had previously accepted, of a summit meeting in the U.N. Security Council to consider the critical situation in the Middle East.

Why the reversal?

"Will I sit down at the same table with that political corpse, Chiang Kai-shek?" he queried. "No, I'll never do it."

There was more of the same, expressed with colorful vigor, and I felt that his trip to Peiping had made very clear Red China's objection to his presence at a meeting of the Security Council where the Formosa government represents China.

But I'm sure that wasn't the only reason for his sudden change of position. Rejecting the Security Council as the proper forum and citing the similar views of General de Gaulle and Walter Lippmann, he proposed first a summit meeting of the great powers to deal with "the whole range of questions." And when I said that was obviously impractical, he proposed a special meeting of the General Assembly "with all countries participating, to condemn the aggressors and demand the withdrawal of their troops" from Lebanon and Jordan.

I suppose he was fearful that any such condemnation

would be voted down overwhelmingly in the Security Council, and he asserted that even unofficial big-power talks which he wants so badly had been excluded by Mr. Dulles unless, as he put it, "they took place by accident in the men's room." It was apparent that the General Assembly looked to him like a better forum for a Soviet effort to mobilize opinion against Britain and America.

The Western intervention to protect Lebanon and Jordan in one respect was probably a welcome relief to Mr. Khrushchev. It diverted world attention from eastern Europe, where only a few weeks earlier the shocking execution of Imre Nagy had dramatized the tightening noose around the satellite empire and called forth a chorus of criticism. Now, suddenly, not Russia but the Americans were on the defensive and Mr. Khrushchev showed a quick and obvious resolve to exploit the situation as best he could.

Throughout this lengthy discussion of procedure in regard to the Middle East, he disclosed a lively concern for public opinion. He said we had antagonized the Arabs by the intervention in Lebanon and added, "Of course, if a country wants to go to war, then it can ignore public opinion. But if one does not want war, then one must take account of public opinion."

When I said that peace depends on the security of all nations from outside interference, that we were not in Lebanon to please Arab opinion but to protect an Arab country at its request, he said he was "astonished" and "surprised," and that "public opinion must be respected."

"See how far we stand from one another," he added in a melancholy tone, "at opposite poles."

I could hardly believe my ears—the Prime Minister of the Soviet dictatorship, which tolerates no criticism, was lecturing me on democracy and the sovereignty of public opinion! But I think he was saying something significant —the present leadership of the U.S.S.R. does consider opinion, for its foreign policy relies, in part at least, on persuasion rather than coercion alone as in Stalin's day.

Our talk ranged over many subjects besides the Middle East—trade between the United States and the Soviet Union, economic aid for the underdeveloped countries, the satellites, Western anxiety about Soviet objectives, etc. But always Khrushchev brought the talk back to his question: "How shall we improve our political relations?"

We found ourselves in hearty agreement on one broad general principle which should govern the conduct of the great powers: No interference in the affairs of smaller countries. But I'm afraid we were "at opposite poles" again in our ideas of what constitutes interference.

I raised, for example, the recent stern Soviet behavior toward the satellites as an illustration of why there is tension and fear in the West of Soviet intentions. Mentioning the current Soviet campaign against what is called "revisionism," and the retreat from his earlier liberal idea of "many roads to socialism," I asked why Soviet policy had grown rigid and Stalinist again. We in America, I went on, feel that all nations should have the right to go in any direction they wish, and are disturbed when we see this right interfered with, even inside the Communist world.

Mr. Khrushchev's manner hardened. He expressed surprise at my interest in ideological disputes "since the capitalists do not consider it possible to build a Communist society." But he quickly added, "No interference in the internal affairs of other countries—let us write that rule down and approve it at a summit conference. We want to establish it and hold it sacred, for these affairs should only be settled by the peoples concerned."

When I asked if that had been the Soviet Union's attitude at the time of the armed intervention in Hungary and the recent denunciation of Tito and Yugoslavia, he let me have it. Following the familiar Communist debating tactic of attack, Mr. Khrushchev assailed the United States and its actions around the world—in Lebanon, Jordan, Guatemala—even Cuba!

"The trouble is that Americans poke their noses where they shouldn't," he complained.

The question had struck a sensitive chord. "I am sure," he went on, "that neither Tito nor Kadar authorized Mr. Stevenson to raise this question. If I wrote Comrade Tito [and he emphasized the word Comrade], he would undoubtedly be deeply shocked, and all the more so would Comrade Kadar, for these are internal matters."

As for Hungary, he went on to say that he was planning to spend his summer vacation with the head of the present Hungarian government, Kadar, and would tell him about my "solicitude" for Hungary.

Then, as though expressing an afterthought, he added, "Let's go together and we will speak to the Hungarian people together and set forth our respective positions to them, and we'll see which position the people will support."

To this I had to reply, "I am afraid that the Hungarian government I am talking about cannot speak any more." And that ended our discussion on Hungary.

He ended the whole subject of the Communist bloc impatiently. "It would be better not to raise questions which relate solely to us and the foreign Communist parties. We and Tito are Communists, and somehow we will settle this affair. It is an internal affair, and in any event you couldn't help us. Let's rather talk about questions of how best to improve relations between us and the United States."

By implication at least, he was saying that whatever goes on in the Communist world is a family affair and doesn't concern outsiders, that Soviet suppression of the uprising in Hungary in 1956 was not "interference" and that Soviet pressure on Yugoslavia to conform to Moscow is not a case of meddling in another country's affairs. But he also made it clear that what happens in the non-Communist world (the "capitalist" world) *is* a proper concern of the Soviet Union. It is hard for us to believe that Russia is afraid of the United States. But I think the Soviet leaders at least really are. And certainly American security measures are uppermost among Russia's fears. "We see ourselves encircled by your bases," Mr. Khrushchev said. "There are no Soviet troops in the Near and Middle East, but the Americans have bases in England, Turkey, Greece, and I don't know where they don't have them. What would you Americans think if we set up bases in Mexico, or some such place? How would you feel?"

The policy of Mr. Dulles, he went on, is one of "rollback." "But history will roll him back. The policy of rollback must be rolled back. You cannot roll us back. On this basis there not only cannot be friendship, there cannot even be good relations."

I told Mr. Khrushchev what he knows full well—that the bases represent only a response to our fear of postwar Soviet ambitions. And, while I wanted to hear Mr. Khrushchev talk rather than myself, I thought it best to briefly put the record straight. So I also reminded him that after the war, in which we had fought Hitler as allies, we genuinely believed in continuing co-operation. We almost totally disarmed, offered to share the atomic secret with the world, gave up the Philippines and pressed hard for an effective United Nations, a work in which I was personally engaged after the war.

But then came a whole series of disillusioning events— Soviet pressure on Greece and Turkey, the coup in Czechoslovakia, the division of Germany, Soviet subjugation of all eastern Europe from the Baltic to the Black Sea, the war in Korea, arms to Egypt. I said our policy had not been aggressive or expansive, but to defend our security and the right of all countries to go their own way, unmolested and secure.

"Mr. Premier," I concluded, "there should be no conflicts between us. We each have enough territory and resources. Our troubles arise from the outside. Maybe we Americans have made mistakes, but this is the way we see things, and I'm sure that my countrymen are very eager to find a way to settle the conflicts that divide us."

"This I believe," Mr. Khrushchev answered, and paid me a pretty compliment. "I have read your speeches. Some things in them are wrong and even offensive [sounded like campaign time at home!], but on the whole I think you stand for improving relations and we welcome it." And then he went on to say something about Soviet attitudes that I think is little understood among us Americans.

He stated frankly and confidently that the world is inexorably going Communist.

"You must understand, Mr. Stevenson, that we live in an epoch when one system is giving way to another. When you established your republican system in the eighteenth century the English didn't like it. Now, too, a process is taking place in which the peoples want to live under a new system of society; and it is necessary that one agree and reconcile himself with this fact. The process should take place without interference. If this principle [of non-interference] were accepted, it would improve the international climate and we would welcome it. But you are playing the part of a gendarme again—in the Middle East."

Thus, the prescription given me by the leader of the

Soviet Union appears to be that events inside the Communist world are none of our business, but the non-Communist world must stand aside while his "new system of society" exploits the nationalist awakening and social unrest in the world, and spreads from country to country.

Perhaps I misunderstood him. I hope so, because such an outlook leaves little hope for the better relations and increasing confidence that are indispensable to peace, security and disarmament.

Moreover, he is wrong. The peoples of the small countries of eastern Europe did not choose Communism; it was imposed on them by the Red Army at the end of the war. The Czech people did not want to live under that system; they were victims of a Communist coup in 1948 —and the atmosphere of suppression there, as I have observed it, bears mute testimony to this fact even now, a decade after.

Communism has had its way in Europe only by force and conspiracy, not by choice. The nationalism and the social unrest in so many parts of the world aren't a Communist revolution. They are a revolt against foreign domination, feudalism and misery. And Communism isn't the way to national independence either, as the Soviet satellites can testify. Moreover the new Russian Empire is a jail—you can't get out once you're in—as Hungary bears witness. Just now we live in hope that the peoples of the Middle East may not have to learn that lesson the hard way.

And I might have added that social reform was not a Soviet monopoly; that they had evidently been so busy trying to make their system work they had overlooked the vast changes in Western society—the redistribution of wealth, growth of industrial democracy and the new concepts of social responsibility. But I have a hunch they don't want to see what has happened in the West which makes so much of their Marx-Lenin bible obsolete and idiotic.

Here I must add that Khrushchev envisages the further expansion of Communism as a peaceful process. No hint of war or the old fire and brimstone rhetoric ever entered the talk.

Russia is changing, too, and memories of the horror of the last war are still fresh. At all events "peace and friendship" was on every official lip and was the burden of the greeting from the good-natured crowds in public places everywhere we traveled. Khrushchev was no exception. As I have said, I would not be surprised if he was as afraid of us as we are of them. After all, economic development and improved living standards are the first priority in Russia, and the rapid progress envisioned in the seven-year plan is dependent on peace. And Khrushchev's idea of Communist expansion by non-violent means, through what he calls "competition of the two systems," may account for the new sensitivity of Soviet foreign policy to world public opinion.

But this report of my lively conversation with him would be incomplete if I failed to mention the lighter moments. At one stage Mr. Khrushchev confided in me that when the leaders of the Communist countries get together, they always toast their best friend, the American Secretary of State, Mr. Dulles. "We say: We will regret it if President Eisenhower's sputnik leaves the State Department, for he helps us so. We'll hardly get a more helpful opponent."

I replied that we Democrats might have to deprive them of that advantage at the next election, and he asked me some questions about American politics.

"But," he said, "you have not shown that there are any differences in foreign policy between your party and Mr. Knowland's" (his name for the Republican party, not mine!).

I felt quite proud of my firm defense of the Republican administration, and assured him that, while there were many differences between us, on some things we Americans were united, including our anxiety about the dangers of war and our desire, regardless of domestic politics, to reduce the tensions and reach agreements.

When I said that improving relations was a two-way street, a process of give-and-take, he said that in the Soviet Union they have always respected America and American culture. And, pointing to a spot midway on the table, he laughed. "Let's meet there, as Churchill said, halfway."

I said we had already gone pretty far to meet him, and again he returned to his favorite topic of talks. Chancellor Raab of Austria had just been there, he said. "A 'little capitalist,' as he called himself, and I, a Communist, found common ground, had a useful talk and parted with feelings of mutual respect and improved relations between our countries. Why can't the same be true of our relations with the United States?"

He mentioned talking about corn and drinking brandy with Mr. Garst* of Iowa in the Crimea and what an agreeable and profitable experience it had been. Pointing to some fine ears of field corn at the end of the room, I said it wasn't bad, but in Illinois where I lived we raised much better corn, and that perhaps we ought to have a summit meeting in a corn field. He approved the idea with delight.

The meeting ended on a positive note—his approval of and, I thought, grave interest in my suggestion that joint recognition of equality of power between us might change the political climate and help arrest "the awful waste of the arms race." The awful "danger, too," he added thoughtfully.

Then he sent for my sons, Borden and John Fell, who were exploring the Kremlin, and a photographer. While the pictures were being taken he talked gaily to the boys. His youngest son, Borden's age, was working in the field of rocket launching, he said proudly. When I mumbled something banal about launching doves of peace, he nodded a solemn, "yes, yes," and said that his older son, a flier, was first wounded and later killed in the war.

* Roswell Garst, a hybrid corn producer of Coon Rapids, Iowa, visited Khrushchev in Russia in 1955. Ed.

Then, jovial again, he suggested that my sons come back and marry Russian girls—"that would be a contribution to Russian-American relations!"

The boys were noncommittal.

While this long and interesting talk, which I have only briefly summarized, was not encouraging about early settlement of any major issues, I didn't come away without hope. I take heart in Khrushchev's desire to avoid war, his ready response to the concept of equality of power between Russia and America and, above all, in his obvious eagerness to talk. And there are other places than summits to talk.

Perhaps it is time to make a gesture, difficult though it may be, a gesture that rejects their system but accepts the chance of decreasing the tensions.

Perhaps, indeed, we should show Mr. Khrushchev, if he wants to see it, how tall the corn grows in Illinois. . . .

The Communist World—a House Divided

WHAT is the situation in the Communist camp? What is the condition of Stalin's empire five years after Stalin's death?

I have observed that Premier Khrushchev and his colleagues in the Kremlin think of the Communist world in exclusive terms—that what goes on there is no concern of ours. But it is a very great concern of theirs, a greater concern indeed than the better relations with the West which Mr. Khrushchev says he wants so badly—and does so little to get, as we see things.

By Stalin's empire I mean, of course, that vast expanse from Albania and East Germany to China. Here live more than a third of the earth's people under the rule of a dozen Communist one-party states "headed"— as the formula runs—by the Soviet Union. It is a political anachronism—a mighty structure of empire in the century of the decline and fall of empires.

Stalin built it as an empire, a greater empire than the Czars'. And Stalin ran it as an empire, reducing once independent countries to mere provinces of the Soviet state in all but name. Then came Nikita Khrushchev's experiment in partial liberalization, reconciliation with

Tito and "de-Stalinization"—and the explosive results that followed in the Hungarian rebellion and the Polish "October" of 1956.

Premier Khrushchev also introduced a new name for the Soviet bloc—"Commonwealth of Socialist Nations" —which suggested a change of relations within the bloc. But reimposition of discipline, re-emphasis of Russia's hegemony over the bloc and violent attacks on "revisionism" have since become the watchword of Soviet policy. Tito has been anathematized all over again, Nagy and other Hungarian patriots have been executed, and today an uneasy calm reigns over the Eastern scene.

Like all empires of diverse peoples, the Communist world is full of contradictions and discords. And it is small wonder that there are recurrent symptoms of trouble in a body so large. The great question mark is Red China and Russo-Chinese relations. The China of Mao Tse-tung plays a very important, perhaps decisive, part in the internal and external politics of the Communist world.

But the "brooding presence" of China along so much of the Soviet borders isn't all the anxious rulers in the Kremlin have to worry about. Marshal Tito declared his independence of Moscow ten long years ago, and we know about the riots in East Germany in 1953, the gallant, tragic fight for freedom in Hungary, and the "October revolution" in Poland in 1956.

I advise everyone who goes to Russia these days to stop in Poland on the way home. For it will free your mind of the notion that the lands behind the Curtain are all alike. I spent several days in Warsaw and then drove south with my sons through the pleasant Polish countryside (where the machine has not yet replaced the horse) to Krakow, that lovely medieval city which was spared by the war. We spent a night at the mountain resort of Zakopane, and went on over the beautiful High Tatras to Bohemia and historic Prague.

But it required only a few hours in Warsaw to make us realize that Poland today is a Communist country with a difference. The first thing that strikes you is Warsaw itself; miraculously the ancient, beautiful city has risen from its ashes. Methodically destroyed, building by building, by the Nazis, it is being rebuilt, stone by stone, by loving Poles—exactly as it was. You walk about restored Warsaw in hushed and awe-stricken respect for this monument to a people's pride, sentiment and indomitable courage. And the unrestored "Ghetto" will long be a terrible reminder of the horrible massacre of a half million Jews.

In Poland you breathe a strikingly different political air from that of Russia or the other satellites. In eastern Germany, for example, mounting Communist pressure was reaching the explosion point last summer and twenty thousand people were escaping to the West each month. But in Poland the pressure has been relaxed since the bloodless revolution of 1956, which scared the Russians and brought Wladyslaw Gomulka out of jail and into power. Gomulka's truce with the church is uneasy, but

Poland is still the "most Catholic country in Europe," and one hour of compulsory religious instruction a day is given in the schools. The bulk of the land has been de-collectivized and has reverted to private farming, with a large increase in production and food supply. Some private trade is permitted and small private retail stores are numerous, if not very prosperous. Emigration is possible and contacts with the West in some fields are being actively encouraged by the regime.

But the main gain of Poland's "October" is in freedom of speech. Freedom of publication does not exist, but people feel free to speak their minds, even to foreigners, as they did to me. In the schools, the Russian language is no longer compulsory, and the required university course in "Marxism-Leninism" has been abandoned in favor of the traditional subjects of philosophy and sociology. There are even sixty-five non-Communists in the Parliament, and criticism and dissent from government policy are not unknown. Poles again enjoy equality before the law, restraints on the secret police have been established and they claim there isn't a single political prisoner any longer.

Political anecdotes are rife, like the one about the monstrous Palace of Culture, Stalin's gift in the middle of Warsaw: the best view of Warsaw, they say, is the one from the Palace, because it is the only place in Warsaw from which you can't see the Palace. As we drove past it one time a witty official murmured to me, "Small but in good taste, don't you think?"

In Poland today they say, "All we need is a new geography." For Poland is sandwiched in between two big powers which have abused her for centuries. For their Russian "liberators" there is historical mistrust and dislike. For the Germans the fear and hatred are still intense in a country where five millions were slaughtered. Warsaw abounds in plaques, always decked with fresh flowers: "Here the Nazis shot as hostages the Poles whose names are listed below: . . ."

With Russia on one side and Germany on the other, it is no wonder that Poles, even high Communist Poles, talk to you about the desirability of lessening international tensions. And they deeply resented our government's casual indifference to the plan for nuclear "disengagement" advanced last spring by Adam Rapacki, Poland's able Foreign Minister. This was the first independent initiative in foreign policy in Moscow's family, and, as such, they felt it deserved more consideration.

Even though Poland is "no more Communist than France," as many say, she is very much at Russia's mercy and her leaders will avoid trouble with Big Brother either from necessity or conviction. Gomulka is a convinced Communist. While he is said to dislike police terror and Russian domination as much as free enterprise and a free press, Gomulka's independence of Moscow is limited. And with West Germany rearming and his Oderneisse frontier still in doubt, the echoes of 1956 are getting fainter and he seems to be returning to the Soviet fold with few reservations.

Russia is also Poland's most important trading partner, and Poland is dependent on Russia for iron ore, oil and cotton. She wants more credits from the U.S. to buy farm products and machinery to build up her consumer goods industries. In poor Poland, where many are driven to steal to live, the emphasis has shifted toward light industry to improve living standards, in contrast to Russia where the emphasis is still largely on basic industry.

The Polish officials seem quite aware that Gomulka's echoes of Russian attacks on the United States are hardly endearing to us. And they point out that their difficulties are further increased on the Russian side when Congress debates credits and aid to Poland as an anti-Communist and anti-Russian gesture, which can only arouse Russian suspicion and imperil the independence already won.

Just before leaving Poland I asked a distinguished scholar, Is Poland free? "No, half-free," was his answer and it sums up the situation pretty well. It is hard to make Communists of Poles: they are too Catholic and they have a sense of humor. But, situated that way, they can't be free either, until Russia lets go. So Poland walks a tightrope, and few Poles would do anything to endanger the national independence and individual liberty attained since 1956 that are always in peril if Moscow tightens the screws.

The Communist governments in eastern Europe are minority governments everywhere. In Poland the solid Communist foundation may not exceed 10 per cent. In Czechoslovakia it is larger, and the industrious Czechs seem to have accepted their fate patiently. They eat well, live better than anyone behind the Curtain and keep still. The atmosphere in passive Prague is oppressive and in sharp contrast to outspoken Poland. And you quickly hear the story about the Czech dog that asked the Polish dog at the border why he was going to Czechoslovakia. "To buy a pair of your fine shoes," said the Polish dog. "And why are you going to my country?" "So I can bark," replied the Czech dog.

If there is more anxiety in Moscow about Poland than Czechoslovakia, there should be still more about East Germany. After Khrushchev gave the hated dictator, Walter Ulbricht, his blessing early last summer, the communizing pressure was steadily increased, and with it the exodus to West Germany—especially of doctors, scientists and professors. Eight hundred doctors alone, almost 20 per cent of all East Germany's physicians, fled in the first eight months of last year. The cream of East Germany's intelligence was draining away and the tension rose so rapidly and dangerously that the Communist bosses took fright and began to ease the pressure last fall.

The possible consequences of a new East German revolt are not overlooked in Moscow. We can only surmise what the West Germans would do. And if they joined their anti-Communist Eastern brothers, what would the Red Army do? And then the Western powers? To stop the hemorrhage from East Germany, and to force recognition and increase the prestige of the puppet government, certainly underlies the renewed Soviet pressure to drive us from Berlin—that tiny, insecure island of freedom and refuge in the Communist ocean.

So all is not sweetness and light in the Communist camp, and Yugoslavia is not Moscow's only headache. Doubtless Poland, East Germany, Hungary and perhaps others contribute to the uneasiness in the Communist corral.

CHAPTER III

Red China—Number One Soviet Problem

WHEN, even between neighbors like Poland and Czechoslovakia, Communist conviction and loyalty to their Moscow masters varies so widely, it is clear that we Americans make a great mistake to treat all the Communist countries alike. They aren't. And to treat them alike only contributes to their solidarity. The fever chart of dissent differs from country to country. In short, Tito and his idea that you can be a good Communist in Yugoslavia and not subservient to Russia is not the Kremlin's only anxiety.

And the biggest anxiety of all is China. In 1957 Mao Tse-tung echoed Khrushchev's earlier liberal ideas about "many roads to socialism." Mao's colorful Chinese equivalent was "let a hundred flowers bloom, and one hundred schools of thought contend." But the results frightened him—a thousand flowers quickly bloomed. And the liberal experiment with dissent was brief; Mao quickly threw his ponderous weight violently against dissent, against Tito, against relaxation of tensions, and for rigid intolerance of any Communist deviation.

And when the leaders of 600,000,000 Chinese speak, Moscow listens. Illustrations are numerous. My own visit with Premier Khrushchev in the Kremlin was only a few hours after he had returned from a secret four-day visit to Peiping. There, I suspect, he heard some vigorous advice about Soviet deportment in the U.N., where "China," as represented by Chiang Kai-shek, agreed to give the Chinese nuclear weapons and promised full support to new efforts to liquidate Formosa and humiliate the U.S.

At one point in my travels last summer I was very near the Chinese border. That was at Alma-Ata (which means "father of apples"), the capital of Kazakhstan, way out in Central Asia, and about as far as you can get around the world from Libertyville, Illinois. Alma-Ata is a beautiful city at the foot of great snow-capped mountains. On the other side is China.

But the presence of China in Russian affairs is something I felt everywhere in the U.S.S.R.—at Tashkent in Uzbekistan, where the huge "Lenin" stadium (they are always named "Lenin" or "Stalin") was festooned with banners welcoming Chinese athletes of the "brotherly republic"; at Sverdlovsk in the heart of the Urals, where packing crates in the great Uralmash heavy machinery works bore Manchurian addresses; and not least in Moscow, where Chinese faces are common and China is very much on the minds of important officials.

As I said, Mao's famous "hundred flowers" were never allowed to bloom; instead, I was told in Moscow, ten thousand little pig-iron blast furnaces have sprouted up over the Chinese landscape using local materials and the limitless labor. In Moscow they speak of the pace of China's industrialization with near awe. A high Polish official told us that Chinese industrial production rose by 30 per cent last year. "Astonishing" was the term Mr. Khrushchev used, and he added that the Chinese themselves had not foreseen the rapidity of the development.

I was entertained at luncheon one day by Mr. Vasili Kuznetsov, the able, attractive acting Foreign Minister while Mr. Gromyko was on vacation. He had served as Soviet Ambassador to China, and had just accompanied Premier Khrushchev on the quick trip to Peiping. He told me that China's iron and steel production will total 9- or 10,000,000 tons this year, equaling France. Next year, he went on, the target is 20,000,000 tons—the British figure!

The story of the economic development of Communist China is not for me to recount. I haven't been there. But I can report that some Russians are emotional about what China has accomplished.

I talked about it one night to Serge Obraztsov, brilliant, ebullient director of the famous Puppet Theater. (And I agree emphatically with my friend John Gunther that if I had one night to spend in Moscow I would spend it at this incomparable entertainment.)

"Every day," he said, "I sit in my theater and dream about the play I am going to do tomorrow and I am happy. That is the way it is with the Russian people. There are many things that we do not have. But happiness does not lie in the things one has. One may have a house, a car, plenty of food—many things—but these do not make happiness. Happiness does not lie in today but in tomorrow—and in our dreams for tomorrow.

"You are a young country, and you are dreaming of tomorrow. We are younger still—only forty-one years old—and we are dreaming of tomorrow. But China is younger than either of us—barely ten years old. It is the youngest, most exciting nation in the world—with the greatest dreams of all. I visited China five years ago. It was the most extraordinary experience of my life. People in China have had nothing—nothing! Now several hundred million people are dreaming of tomorrow. I cannot describe to you the feeling of excitement there— much, much more even than here in the Soviet Union."

But with the pride there is also anxiety about what China's industrial development means for the future. One day I asked a high official, who must be nameless, "And how about the production of babies in China?" adding that if the Chinese population continues to expand at the present rate, Russia will one day look to her neighbor like the "largest, emptiest land in the world."

"Ah, that's the trouble," he replied unhesitatingly. The question in my mind—and, I think, in his—was: What will Russia's position be when a powerful, industrialized China, bursting with population, begins to eye the vast and sparsely populated reaches of the Russian land?

And whenever I remarked, as I often did, that a U.N. commission estimated the population of China in the year 2000 at 1.6 billion the look of consternation was invariable. Nor was I surprised when on a couple of occasions Soviet officials quickly raised their vodka glasses and replied, "Which is another reason for better Soviet-American relations."

Having all this in mind, I asked Anastas Mikoyan, First Deputy Premier and the leading authority on trade, about Soviet-Chinese economic relations. "Never any friction," he assured me. Russian-Chinese trade is said to be about $1,500,000,000 annually, and principal Russian exports are machinery, metals and oil. But what was Russia importing from China in return for its exports, I asked.

Mikoyan mentioned silk, rice, blankets, bed sheets and other items. The Soviet Union, he said, makes it a practice to take what China can supply. For example, we produce much silk but still can absorb some 12,000,000 meters from China. Sometimes, he went on, we reduce our own output of a given commodity by 2 or 3 per cent in order to accommodate imports from China. We have deliberately shifted part of our rice acreage in Central Asia to cotton in order to be able to absorb a large amount of Chinese rice.

Was this trade conducted on a money basis? Yes, he said, within a framework of credit relations. Individual organizations in both countries deal on a monetary basis and at the end of the year there's a clearing arrangement. If total trade does not balance out, "additional deliveries" must be made the next year. The Chinese could, according to present arrangements, go into debt to Russia for as much as 300,000,000 rubles ($80,000,000 at the official rate of exchange), but if the debt went any higher it was necessary to "talk things over."

But "never any friction," he repeated.

I wonder! Certainly relations have not always been as warm as they appear to be now.

But—and this is the "word for today"—it would be a very great mistake to underestimate the present solidarity of Russia and China—or, indeed, as Khrushchev implied, of the whole Communist empire. They may fight like cats and dogs with each other, but as far as the outside world is concerned their unity is formidable. They will stick together. Theirs is one universe; ours is another. The Polish Foreign Minister used the analogy of a family where emotional arguments at home don't mean disunion outside.

And any idea that Russia and China especially can be divided is dangerous fantasy, at least for the present.

In Paris, Pierre Mendès-France, the former Prime Minister of France, who recently visited China, confirmed this emphatically. And he went on, with sober gravity, to confirm another impression: the angry hostility of the Chinese leaders to the U.S. and the intensity of the "hate-America" campaign.

China is the oldest, the largest and was once the greatest nation on earth. The Chinese feel, I was told, that they have been humiliated by the West for generations and that they still are being humiliated by the United States, which refuses to acknowledge their revolution, insists that the island of Formosa is the legitimate China, keeps them out of the United Nations and is forever plotting war against them.

I wonder if we Americans realize how bitter—"explosive" was Mendès-France's word—this feeling is. And the threatening, intemperate tone Khrushchev and Co. use about Formosa suggests that the Russians are going to leave no doubt—especially in Peiping—about their support of China's claims to Formosa.

Friends in Europe, anxious about the bitterness in China, urged me to go there, not to learn about China but to try to explain our side—that we are not bloodthirsty conspirators waiting to destroy them and restore Chiang Kai-shek, that we too have grievances that we feel very deeply, that we worry about their intentions as much as they worry about ours, and that all we want is peace and a just settlement of the future of Formosa in accordance with the wishes of the Formosans.

I thanked them all kindly for suggesting such a mission, and said that, after traveling so much, I was glad Americans couldn't go to China—almost!

CHAPTER IV

Russia Wants More U. S. Trade

LAST year Soviet trade reached large proportions. Deputy Premier Anastas Mikoyan told me it was over $8,000,-000,000. Trade, like production, is controlled by the state and costs (which we can't accurately compute) do not decide prices as in private business. Consequently Communist trade can be managed to serve political as well as economic ends. For example, Russia can take commodities which others may have trouble selling—Iceland's fish, Ceylon's rubber, Uruguay's wool, etc. And she does, with political consequences long foreseen and now apparent.

It is reliably reported that the Communist trade and aid drive has won important economic footholds in some nineteen countries from Argentina to Indonesia. There are other reasons for this penetration, including long-term low-interest credits, liberal currency provisions and low prices. Russian oil has even invaded the Western Hemisphere—in exchange for Argentine wool, Brazilian coffee and Chilean copper—and at cut-rate prices. Soviet aluminum, tin, platinum and zinc exports have depressed world markets. But most East-West trade is conducted at world prices.

United States trade with the Communist bloc is negligible, less than one-half per cent of our exports last year.

Russia is eager for more trade with us. I talked about this with Khrushchev and at length with Mikoyan, the sharp Soviet trade expert and the only top leader who has survived all the bloody purges and convulsions in the Kremlin.

Premier Khrushchev was irritated that the full text of his letter to President Eisenhower last June proposing a large increase in trade had not been published in the United States. When he added that therefore they could not publish the President's "good reply" for "prestige reasons" you get a glimpse of how touchy they are.

I said he could hardly expect to get new credits from the United States until the Lend-Lease account from the last war was settled on some reasonable basis. He quickly agreed, and added that any such settlement would be only a small part of what we were spending on "anti-Soviet propaganda" and on credits to our allies "to maintain strained East-West relations." This *non sequitur* was quickly followed by the old Soviet argument that comparative sacrifices must be considered—"all the fathers, sons and brothers who died in the war"—in settling their Lend-Lease obligation for all the war materials we sent them during the war. I was tempted to remind Mr. Khrushchev that Russia was allied with Hitler until he turned on them and that their awful losses were suffered not to help us but in self-defense.

He went on to say that he really didn't expect American credits; that American aid, as the case of West Germany showed, was not a matter of expenditure but political policy. Likewise, he said, while America criticizes Soviet concentration on heavy industry at the expense of consumer goods it won't help us improve the situation by developing, for instance, our chemical industry. Khrushchev's conclusion was that "the Russian people now see that Americans are not really concerned about their welfare but are pursuing political aims of their own."

I wonder if they always charge us with political motives for everything because they always have one? And these curious little contortions of fact to fit everything into a pattern of American malevolence revealed again the obstacles on the road to that mutual "trust" which Khrushchev says we must establish.

Mr. Mikoyan is a slight, dark, sharp Armenian, and eager for more trade with us. I asked him some questions and he was off.

Soviet foreign trade last year was over $8,000,000,000; and the Soviet Union could find $500,000,000, or $600,-000,000, or even $1,000,000,000 to trade with the United States. "Back in 1931, Soviet-U.S. trade reached $600,-000,000 at prices of that time. Now the Soviet economy is much more developed, and our output is increasing at 11 per cent to 12 per cent a year," he told me.

When I asked him what goods they could exchange in such volume, he said, "The goods will appear when interest appears; certain branches of our industry could be expanded still more rapidly if the U.S. showed interest in trade. But," he concluded, "trade would be virtually impossible unless present discriminatory practices were abandoned."

There followed a recital of grievances; visa difficulties, discriminatory tariffs, export licensing, concluding with this: "Your system of export licensing for everything is very bureaucratic. The Soviet Union is also plagued with bureaucracy, but in this you surpass us." It was about the only concession I got in Russia.

When I asked him what they wanted most from us, he mentioned textile and chemical machinery, equipment for paper factories, and referred to other items in Khrushchev's letter to the President. He was very pleased by a recent deal with an American company for chemical equipment. While he thought that businessmen of the two countries "got along quite well together," Mikoyan said President Roosevelt's slogan was "live without fear," but evidently American firms were living in fear of trading with the U.S.S.R.

Trade is very much on the minds of the Russian industrialists and about the only visible bad temper I saw in the U.S.S.R. was the manager of a machine tool factory in Siberia who exploded, "What sort of a national policy is it not to trade!" He revealed the extreme irritation of the Russians who have been forced at great effort, expense and economic inconvenience to build plants to make machinery they could buy abroad cheaper and quicker.

Mikoyan touched on the same point. "We might want to buy some excavators in the U.S. over a year or so to help with our canal-building program." "But," I said, "I've seen the largest excavators in the world in the great Uralmash plant in the Urals." "True," he answered, "but our plants are working at capacity, and when we need still more excavators temporarily we would rather buy them than expand our production and create useless capacity."

I doubt if very much excess capacity has been built which would have been unnecessary had postwar trade relations with the West been normal. But some diversion of labor, materials and skills painfully needed for war repair and development is certainly part of the price they have paid for dividing the world and, incidentally, encouraging an earlier Chinese adventure—the attempt to take Korea.

To my questions about Soviet attitudes on economic self-sufficiency, Mikoyan said, with smiling sarcasm, that they took into account the statements of "brave generals of yours about wiping the Soviet Union off the face of the earth," and wanted to be independent of the "capitalist world" in the basics. To depend on foreign sources for, say, 5 per cent to 10 per cent of a given machine, Mikoyan said, would not impair that independence.

"We are for trade!" he repeated. "You can produce some things more cheaply than we can, and we should expand output of the items we can produce more cheaply." He said they had lots of timber, paper, cellulose to sell, "even to the United States," and that they wanted to sell oil and minerals in Europe, probably in competition with the United States.

"Competition" brought me to the recent Russian cut-rate sales not only of oil but of tin, zinc and especially aluminum. Was this economic warfare? Was it to demoralize world markets? Did they have surplus aluminum? What were their future intentions?

His reply was interesting. First, it was not economic warfare; they export aluminum mainly to get foreign exchange. "For example, the Soviet Union exported twenty thousand tons to Britain to pay for goods bought there. Had we not needed the British currency we would have used the aluminum because our domestic requirements are growing, or we would have stockpiled it—it doesn't spoil."

And then he added that Russia was forced to enlarge its aluminum industry when the United States insisted that aluminum was a strategic material and persuaded Europe not to sell to the U.S.S.R. "And now we have a comical situation; the Soviet Union is selling aluminum to the very countries that are forbidden to sell to the Soviet Union. Apparently you gentlemen have no sense of humor!" I was inclined to agree. Meanwhile, the U.S.S.R. has already become the third largest producer.

The talk turned to Soviet aid to underdeveloped countries. They have surprised us by the magnitude of their effort in this field: some $2,000,000,000 of small grants and low-interest credits, and scientific-technical agreements with fifteen countries. Since 1955 the Soviets have undertaken about 150 industrial projects; steel and textile mills, bridges, sugar refineries, cement plants, oil exploration, etc. Platoons of technicians help to carry the Communist message to poor people in distant places, especially strategic places. They live at the people's level and often speak their languages. Soviet propaganda attacks the free world's development efforts as "exploitation" and "economic imperialism." And Communist influence is growing.

I asked the able Mr. Mikoyan what they had in mind for the future in this field and later talked with Mr. Skachkov, Chairman of the "Committee on External Economic Relations." I got no inkling that China is unhappy, as many say, about the diversion of Soviet resources to other areas to win friends and influence people. Indeed, China has a modest economic aid program of its own—a highway in Yemen, rice and cloth to Indonesia.

They told me they believe in the international division of labor and that, "since everything is expanding," their economic assistance programs would have to expand too. But I could get no idea of the dimension of the future effort. When I asked if it wouldn't put a severe strain on Soviet resources, Mikoyan said only, "Our shoulders are broad."

My question about the political cancellation of their credit to Yugoslavia touched a sore spot. And Mr. Skachkov politely informed me that the U.S.S.R. had never broken an economic agreement. I gathered that their agreements permit suspension by either party, which

seems to make them merely expressions of intention—
subject to good political behavior.

The subject of aid concluded with Mikoyan's assur-
ances that the Soviet Union was ready to co-operate as
well as compete in economic assistance for the less developed countries. This is something I have urged for
years. The price for them of a pooled effort not identi-
fied with any single country is high—the loss of their
political leverage. If it works, well and good, the project
helps the country's development. If co-operation is impossible, as it may well be, then at least the blame can
be assessed. The Regional Development Agency for the
Middle East, an old proposal now adopted by the Administration, might be a good place to try out a joint
effort at economic and technical assistance.

My interesting talk with Anastas Mikoyan ended, as
most of them did, on politics. He asked me bluntly, but
with a complimentary twist, how one so educated and
informed could make such "groundless attacks on the
Soviet Union in every speech." He asked if it was a political requirement in the U.S.; if conditions made "anti-
Soviet attacks mandatory." With a smile he said he was
reminded of the counterrevolutionary war of 1918-20
when no one made a speech in Russia without attacking
the "entente"—though the people didn't know who or
what it was and thought it was a woman!

Patience isn't always easy in these talks but it is the
best policy if you are trying to get their view of things
rather than express your own. So I resisted the provoca-

New Moscow from the top of the University.

Most of these photographs were taken by John Fell Stevenson, a few by Borden Stevenson. The former are reproduced here by courtesy of Magnum Photos, Inc.

was often told that the fondest wish of every Russian is "a home of my own" and certainly housing is the greatest domestic problem.

I usually had a crowd of mild-mannered, inquisitive and laughing children near by.

The Russians are considerate of nationalist feelings, and the manager of the great textile plant in Uzbekstan in Central Asia is an Uzbek

n Siberia we were always sur-
ounded by crowds of curious and
pplauding workers and peasants.

alin may have been downgraded
Moscow following Khrushchev's
tack, but his image, along with
enin's, is everywhere in the prov-
ces.

In the Baptist church in Moscow the congregation waved white handkerchiefs.

On the collective farms the women work in the fields and orchards like
the men.

was not asking for votes at this
factory gate!

The log houses of old Russia have
not disappeared.

I found the people, old and young alike, courteous, curious and friendly.

Language was no barrier to communication in Russian machine shops.

Maria Kovrigina was until recently the very able Minister of Health of the Soviet Union and one of the women members of the party Praesidium.

The city architect of Sverdlovsk is justly proud of the rebuilding and housing construction program.

Khrushchev, full of amiability, greets John Fell Stevenson. At left is Georgi A. Zhukov, Chairman of the State Committee of Cultural Relations with Foreign Countries.

With my hosts in the Ural Mountains where Europe ends and Asia begins.

There are many huge statues of Lenin like this one in Alma-Ata. In the distant background lies China.

There are toasts to peace and friendship in vodka, wine, champagne and brandy even at picnics—and what a picnic this was on a collective farm in Central Asia.

Millions of acres of virgin land have been planted in Kazakhstan and Siberia in the past few years.

The roads along the Turkestan-Siberia railroad are neither paved nor fenced.

Along the banks of the Volga we saw peasants out of Tolstoy and the past.

The younger leaders are often trained engineers and economists, practical men more interested in production than ideology.

Lunch with the Mufti of Central Asia in Tashkent. The toasts had to be translated from Uzbek to Russian to English, and back. The ripe figs were incomparable.

There are bookstalls everywhere—and reading is the national pastime.

At the Academy of Sciences in Leningrad I talked with some of the highest-paid Soviet citizens—the great scholars and scientists.

The hydroelectric dam on the Ob River in Siberia is on the opposite side of the world from Hudson's Bay and much of the construction was in sub-zero temperatures.

Soviet propaganda leaves nothing to the imagination and not much to credulity.

Huge fast steamers are replacing the old sidewheeler. At Volga River towns between Kazan and Gorky the people make the most of the short summer.

The Kremlin symbolizes the autocracy which cements the old Russia of St. Basil's Cathedral to the new of Lenin's tomb.

tion and replied that I was sure he knew quite well the many reasons for our dislike and mistrust. But, I added, there is one factor in our relations that is very much on my mind—the ignorance of the United States and its motives throughout the Soviet Union.

When I complained about travel restrictions for foreigners, about jamming American broadcasts and censorship of American news reports from Russia, his temper rose.

But we ended that day in good spirits. I said we couldn't always hear what we wanted to hear. Mikoyan agreed that life would be pretty dull that way—and that at least we could agree on more trade. Whereupon he presented me with a huge gift box of all kinds of Russian cigarettes. And I don't smoke.

CHAPTER V

The Russians Like Us

WE LANDED in Leningrad at about the same time the Marines landed in Lebanon. This coincidence colored our whole Russian experience and underlined the fact that while we Americans may not be very popular any more in some parts of the world, they still like us in Russia! By "they" I mean the ordinary people.

As we traveled from Leningrad to Moscow, out to Central Asia, up to Siberia and back through the Urals and along the Volga, the government-controlled radio and press poured out hourly and ugly assaults on United States "imperialism." Yet everywhere we met with courtesy, friendliness and curiosity. The Communist leaders may fear and even hate us. If they do, it is wonderfully concealed and the average Russian's naturally friendly attitude seems to have survived decades of anti-American propaganda. They know little about us, and their few vague ideas are sometimes sadly distorted. But their curiosity and eagerness are disarming.

My photographer son, John Fell, who always had two cameras around his neck, was the center of constant attention. "What kind are they?" "How much did they cost?" "How many pictures can you take?" "Will they really take color?", etc., etc. Some of these chance ac-

quaintances were bold enough to come back to the hotel
to listen, enchanted, to some jazz records he brought
along for presents. Their questions about phonographs,
radio, TV, schools, automobiles, and every aspect of
life in America, were searching and always accompanied
by politeness and dignity.

The hospitality was as unfailing as the courtesy. All my
hosts—Russian, Uzbek, Kazakh, Siberian, Tartar—were
good-humored, proud, eager and inexhaustible. I saw
sights, talked with dignitaries, swallowed insipid fruit
juices, ate endless feasts and drank numberless toasts to
peace and friendship—until I wasn't sure how much
more peace and friendship I could stand! But more than
once I couldn't stand any more food, even at breakfast.
My sons took an inventory of the table one morning at
Alma-Ata near the border of China: raspberries, straw-
berries, apples, grape juice, tomato juice, cucumbers,
bread, caviar, cheese, mare's milk, cow's milk, yogurt,
coffee, tea, sausages, ham, jam, cookies, candy, *pâté*,
pickles, butter, fried potatoes, fried eggs, roast chicken,
cauliflower au gratin—and vodka!

In Leningrad I even talked to the "man on the street"
one evening, something that is not easy to do. It was a
mixed group of students and workers. They had gathered
in front of my hotel, not to see me, but to examine a
strange and wonderful sight—a 1956 Buick. Their hair
was long, their clothes poor, but they were friendly and
good-humored, with a ready laugh when I said we hoped
to go to Siberia—"and also to return." They were in-

tensely curious about America, our education and living conditions. "How many hours of work to buy this car?" stumped me, but my sons saved me. Some of the eager questions reflected, I thought, obvious mistrust of the information the people were getting from their own sources.

When I excused myself to go to bed and left my sons to carry on, I cheerily said something like, "Well, come to see us in America." And the wistful "How?" that greeted me from several eager young men will haunt me a long time.

In Moscow a few days later, the Soviet propaganda machine was running full blast on the Lebanon landing. In diplomatic circles the atmosphere was tense. My old colleague of early U.N. days, Andrei Gromyko, the Soviet Foreign Minister, was friendly and courteous, but unrestrained in his criticism of our action. Meetings were being held in parks and factories to denounce the "American imperialists" and their "attack" on the Arabs. Our able Ambassador, Llewellyn Thompson, foresaw a torrent of abuse and trouble in the street. The newspapers announced that Soviet army units would maneuver in the Caucasus and Central Asia just as we took off—for Central Asia.

"Central Asia"—Turkestan—is a vast area of many peoples larger than all western Europe. It includes five "Republics" in southern Russia, where they try hard to preserve the fiction of national independence while rapidly Russianizing the languages and everything else.

The huge northern Republic of Kazakhstan is the center of Khrushchev's bold plan to plow up millions of acres of virgin land. This vast new frontier is growing rapidly, and the recent immigration from Russia has already reduced the native Kazakhs to a minority. The Kazakhs look Mongolian. But the peoples of the four southern Republics look more like the Turks—who migrated from Central Asia long ago. They are all Moslems, and Russia proudly boasts that she is the fourth Moslem power of the world.

In 1923 Stalin said, "The task is to transform Turkestan into a model Republic, an advanced post for revolutionizing the East." I wanted to see what had happened in Stalin's "show window" to the East. And what I saw were modern industrial cities, huge farms and the last vestiges of timeless, colorful, oriental Turkestan melting into standard Soviet patterns of industrialization and architectural monotony.

Our first stop was Tashkent, capital of the Soviet Republic of Uzbekistan, two thousand miles southeast of Moscow. The official welcome, in a temperature of 110 degrees, couldn't have been more hospitable, and we were whisked away to the country VIP guest house of the City Soviet by cheerful officials busily planning to kill us with kindness. In the car we read the big headlines: "The working people of Uzbekistan are wrathfully protesting the imperialist aggression." But the crowd of working people at the airport smiled broadly and clapped their hands when I waved a greeting.

While the press and radio screamed imprecations and a mob stormed the American Embassy in faraway Moscow, another mob of beaming Uzbeks in their embroidered skullcaps waited outside the mosque in Tashkent to bid us a smiling, cheering good-by after our luncheon with the Mufti. (Nor will I forget that dignitary's toast at lunch when he reminded me of some wise Moslem words: "Believe what you see, not what you hear.")

A few days later at Alma-Ata, the lovely capital of Kazakhstan near the border of China, we read that "all the working people are wrathfully condemning the American aggression against the freedom-loving people of Lebanon." But the working people of Alma-Ata, and everyone else, showed not wrath but warmth.

Near Alma-Ata we had a gigantic picnic in a grove on a collective farm, with mountains of strange foods in front of us and snow-capped mountains behind us. There were toasts by the score to peace and friendship, as always, and a riotous champagne finale. It was another day of "the people's wrath." But when we left if there was anything wrong with our jolly Mongol and Russian hosts, it wasn't wrath!

Nor will I forget other incidents of that journey through remote Turkestan. In ancient Samarkand, where Alexander the Great married the lovely Princess Roxana and Tamerlane ruled the world from the Danube to the China Sea, the news of the little American "invasion" spread quickly. Crowds formed everywhere we went, and I will remember the bursts of applause and the smiling eastern faces of the living people of Samarkand longer even than its noble ruins.

The Middle Eastern crisis certainly aroused fears even in remote Central Asia that events might be drifting toward the war that people in Russia dread as much as we do. I recall especially the worried face of the elderly chairman of a great collective farm, who asked in a low voice, as he was showing me through a children's nursery, if I couldn't "do something." He must have thought I had won the election!

And so it went as we traveled northward into Siberia. The most moving experience of all was in Rubtsovsk, way out on the lonely prairies of Siberia, where they had just held indignation meetings to denounce the wicked American "imperialists." Large crowds seemed to always be in front of my hotel. Reserved and shy at first, they clapped vigorously at my first sign of greeting whenever we appeared.

They haven't seen many Americans in Rubtsovsk and curiosity had much to do with it. Walking through the crowds, joking with the people, which isn't easy in Russian, the handclasps and smiles were eager and warm. The father of a fat baby said, "We've meat and bread and milk up to our necks—what we want is peace." There, as everywhere, the refrain was peace, peace, peace.

And I won't forget a night in Novosibirsk—the largest city of Siberia with the largest theater in the country. After the performance when the audience had applauded the performers they suddenly all wheeled around, faced the center box and applauded—us! It was the end of another day of "wrathful indignation" over America's "aggression."

What accounts for the contrast between the friendly people and the savage propaganda? Why didn't they knock us down instead of embracing us? No one is too confident of the answer. Some Russians say the criticism is just of "your ruling clique." But there must be some immunity to propaganda after forty years of falsehood, and certainly there is an abiding admiration for the United States as the most "advanced" country, and also gratitude for our help in the war.

The contrast is still more surprising when you consider that these people are cut off from outside information which might help them evaluate what they read in their newspapers and hear on their radio—and that is all they can read and hear. We kept a careful log on foreign broadcasts with a short-wave radio. Never once were we able to hear more than the first few seconds of a Russian-language broadcast from the Voice of America, the B.B.C. or even the United Nations before the jamming drowned them out. They go to great trouble and expense to see to it that the people hear only one side of a story and to keep them in ignorance of the United States and its motives.

Later I brought this up with Anastas Mikoyan, and pointed out that on our long journey in the interior every American broadcast in Russian was jammed and the newspapers gave no account of our side of the story about Lebanon; that all press reports from Russia by foreign journalists had been censored for years; that large areas of the country were closed to travel by foreigners (although not to me); and that the hope for peace lay in knowledge and communication, not in ignorance and suppression of both.

His temper rose. If my report was correct and the Voice of America had always been jammed, he said he would send a letter to the Minister of Communications— a letter of congratulation! For America, he said, was waging "a cold war against the Soviet Union," the State Department officially said so, "it was their main line of behavior," and the Soviet Union had to take steps to counteract it. When the cold war ended the jamming would end, and also the travel restrictions, he said, but, as to censorship, the U.S. press frequently "distorts" the facts, "which we don't find too pleasant."

Impetuously I replied that for two weeks I had been reading Russian distortions about America's motives in the Middle East which I didn't find pleasant either. And we were off to Donnybrook again!

Evidently one of the important functions of the Ministry of Communications is to prevent communication. In recent years they have expelled four or five American correspondents, and now they have shut down the C.B.S. bureau in Moscow because of "anti-Soviet" programs.

Russia is a lot of people with a single head, and it is all too plain that the channels of communication must be opened if we are to bring about better understanding and mutual trust. An open world is the indispensable ingredient of peace. And on our return to Moscow from Central Asia and Siberia I ended my statement for the press with the suggestion that if we must compete the best place to begin would be in the spread of truth and not falsehood about each other. The Soviet newspapers reported my long statement in full—minus this suggestion.

But there are hopeful signs too—the growth of person-to-person contact through travel, the exchange visits of students and scholars and specialists, and the expansion of cultural relations under the recent treaty. Another is the enthusiasm of people in Russia for more contact and communication with us. Expressions of this feeling, like the friendliness, met us everywhere. I think of the ragged little boy in the squalid, narrow alleys of an old Central Asian town, who solemnly asked me to take home "friendly greetings to the children of America."

And I also think of the chess instructor in the House of the Young Pioneers in Alma-Ata (sign over the door said: "Thanks to the Party and the Government for Our Happy Childhood") who wanted me to play a game with his best player. When I asked where he was he said, "Taking his nap; you see he's not quite five years old." I got out of there in a hurry! But not before I asked if the prodigy was a Kazakh. No. A Russian? "No— he's a Korean."

After seeing the anti-American headlines and hearing

the radio attacks in a distant place one night, my note-book concludes: "If this has been going on for twenty years it is a wonder that we are still at peace." And it is.

So I take hope, above all, in the horror of war which the Russian people know so well and in the friendly feelings we found everywhere during those "days of the people's wrath."

CHAPTER VI

Russia's Industrial Revolution—the New Managerial Class

THE Russia I saw in 1958 was not the backward peasant nation I saw in 1926, thirty-two years ago. The peasant, the moujik, has been sent to school, put on a tractor or set to work in mines and factories. He is a moujik no longer. The biggest revolution that has occurred in Russia in our lifetime is the industrial revolution.

As I wrote earlier, "Overtake America" is its slogan. You see it on huge red signs in factory yards, even on posters in children's playgrounds. The concentration on development and production is something to behold. By "overtaking" America they mean matching America in per capita production. And it is already almost halfway there. Mr. Khrushchev's new seven-year plan promises the Russians the highest living standard in the world by 1970 or before.

But today's Russia is still a land of sharp and vivid contrasts. You cruise luxuriously down to Central Asia at five hundred miles per hour on great jet airliners that have been standard equipment for more than two years, and there, in Samarkand, bearded old men on donkeys are sauntering along dusty roads—like pictures out of the Bible. In Tashkent, Navoi Street is broad and busy and lined on one side with huge forbidding modern buildings, and on the other side is the "old city," a labyrinth of winding little alleys and low mud brick oriental hovels, unchanged for centuries. Here and there in trellised tea gardens Uzbek men squat on raised platforms, sip their tea and quietly chat as they have done also for centuries.

Traveling on a comfortable old side-wheeler up the Volga from Kazan to Gorky, we docked at dilapidated wooden river towns. On the banks old peasants sold boiled eggs and berries, munched black bread and dried fish and looked like characters out of Tolstoy. Then we visited a huge new hydroelectric dam built by the peasants' sons and rode for many miles on the great river in a boat of the future, a sleek ninety-passenger "hydrofoil rocket" that skims along above the waves on submerged "wings" at fifty miles per hour.

Which is the real Russia—the old or the new? Both are, of course, but I think that we will do well to think of it in terms of the jet airliners and not the donkeys, the hydrofoil boat and not the crumbling river villages, the engineer sons rather than the peasant fathers. For it is this new, changing, expanding Russia of big industry, advanced science and new frontiers, of grandiose plans and prospects, which today confronts us as an ambitious rival.

The Soviets say that their gross national product will soon approximate half of ours and that by 1965 the Communist bloc will produce more than half the world's industrial goods. Much has been written about this rapid development, the emphasis on heavy industry, the neglect of consumer goods, the rate of growth, the successes and failures. Let me just report a few impressions of what I saw from Moscow to mid-Siberia.

In Leningrad the Elektrosila works makes generators up to 150,000 kw. capacity. Among the ten thousand employees are four thousand women. When I say that the symbol of Russia today is "Men Working," I mean women, too. I saw them doing everything from mending roads to forging steel and precision machining.

From the first plant to the last the lay visitor has a feeling of intensity and concentration among the workers, and also inefficiency. Greater efficiency is a universal problem in Soviet industry, which often uses two workers to match the product of one American.

Almost three thousand miles eastward near Novosibirsk, a fast-growing, young city of eight hundred thousand, we saw some of these generators being installed in the most northerly large-scale hydroelectric project in the world. The dam across the Ob River which flows into the Arctic is three miles wide, the first of a series of dams to harness the power of this great waterway. A complete town had been built nearby, and work goes on right through the bitter Siberian winter that lasts from October to May.

But that summer day it was 90 degrees, and our tour ended on a boat on the lake behind the dam—with sturgeon, caviar, champagne and toasts to peace and friendship.

Where will the power go? To supply the industries of

Novosibirsk and to electrify a portion of the Trans-Siberian railroad. How much will the power cost to produce? The figures were meaningless because the government builds the dam and there is no factor for interest or amortization of the investment.

How much do the workers get? One thousand to two thousand rubles per month, or one hundred dollars to two hundred dollars at our tourist rate of exchange. But the salary of our guide, the very able "chief of construction," was the harder to figure. With bonuses but without perquisites, perhaps eighteen thousand dollars a year, and his taxes are only about 6 per cent.

As we left we walked beneath a large signboard inscribed with Lenin's words: "Communism is the Soviet power plus electrification." By 1972 the U.S.S.R. aims to be producing more power than we do now.

But they are suffering from an acute shortage of capital. Although Premier Khrushchev has recently hinted at a cutback in the ambitious and expensive hydroelectric and atomic power program, he promises to invest as much in industry in the next seven years as in the whole forty years of Soviet rule. It seems likely that the spectacular pace of Soviet heavy industry investment will have to slow down at last.

If Novosibirsk was moved to the other side of the world, it would be somewhere in Hudson Bay. But the harsh climate doesn't seem to retard the industrial growth which, like all the interior, got such impetus from the Nazi thrust into European Russia. Here at the Efremov works we saw enormous drills, presses, planers, cutters, pumps. "Because you wouldn't sell to us, we have made our own," an irritable factory manager said to me. And they surely have! The packing crates were labeled for many foreign lands, especially China and North Korea.

In Russian factories you see many American, British and German machines, reminder of the brisk trade of twenty-five years ago and of $15,000,000,000 of American Lend-Lease aid during the war. But now they are making their own, and one by one the old foreign machines are being replaced by modern Soviet tools.

Although Novosibirsk is off limits for foreigners, here as elsewhere our hosts imposed no restrictions on photographs, and my sons, Borden and John Fell, took anything they wished in the factories and out.

But the most interesting thing about Novosibirsk is the "City of Science" which is being built on the Ob River fifteen miles away to house twenty-five thousand. The purpose of this enormous concentration of scientists, institutes and scholars is not just education. That is secondary; the objective is the economic exploration and development of the vast Siberian treasure house where, they say, the industrial output already exceeds the total output of Czarist Russia.

A thousand miles west of Novosibirsk is Sverdlovsk, "capital of the Urals," where Europe ends and Asia begins. A mining center for two hundred years, this old town was formerly called Ekaterinberg, and here in 1918 the exiled Czar and his family were shot in a cellar as the liberating army of the Provisional Siberian government approached from Siberia. We peeked in the house, now a "Party School," but they wouldn't let us see the cellar.

Here, as everywhere, in spite of the strident "Hands off Lebanon" propaganda, the people were friendly and we were entertained violently. Proudly they showed us a gigantic new statue of Lenin, the large Polytechnic Institute and huge new housing developments. I was fascinated by the museum exhibiting the amazing mineral resources of the Urals. The clown and the wild horsemen in the circus I shall never forget, nor the children's puppet theater in the garden of the once great mansion of a mining magnate.

But Sverdlovsk's industry is more important. The "Uralmash" factory, where the last tank built in the war decorates the entrance, employs sixteen thousand to make machinery for heavy industry, including blast furnaces and rolling mills for India. Like most Soviet plants this one works three eight-hour shifts and a forty-six-hour week (six hours on Saturdays). But, following the lead of iron and steel, all Soviet industry is now shifting over to a seven-hour day and forty-one-hour week (six hours on Saturday), and without cutting the wage level.

There seems to be universal agreement between government, management and labor that "productivity must go ahead" of wage increases, to use the phrase of the able director of Uralmash and the equally able chairman of the trade union committee.

But the big news in Russia is Khrushchev's reorganization of industry, which was formerly managed in every
detail from large cumbersome centralized ministries in
distant Moscow. Those fortresses of Stalin's bureaucracy
were disbanded last year under Khrushchev's bold new
scheme for decentralized management of industry, and
now most of Russia's 200,000 enterprises are run by 106
regional economic councils.

We visited some of them. The chief of the council for
the province of Sverdlovsk in the Urals is Sergei Stepanov.
He used to be Minister of Transport Machinery in Moscow. Now, with some thirty other executives who also
formerly worked in Moscow and a staff of one thousand
five hundred, his regional council manages five hundred
factories and construction projects employing 600,000
people in a province about the size of Great Britain. This
council, in turn, is subordinate to the State Planning
Committee, the famous Gosplan, located in Moscow.
The principles of central planning and control are still
at the heart of the Soviet system, but the operational
management has been decentralized.

When I later talked with Mr. Khrushchev, he told me
frankly that the old system of centralized management
was "impossible." You can't run the industry of such a
big country from one center, he said emphatically, adding
that the effort to do it had only caused paralysis, duplica-
tion and waste while able men in the outlying areas sat
around waiting for directives from above. "Now we have

freed ourselves from the routine current work in order to concentrate on the larger problems."

The story was pretty much the same everywhere. As a plant director in Siberia put it, "A factory couldn't even sell a horse without Moscow's permission." At Gorky the young director of an auto plant employing forty-five thousand (formerly called the Molotov works until he fell from political grace) said, "Now I can build what I need when I need it; before I had to get approval from Moscow."

The plant directors and regional council chairmen struck me for the most part as very able. These are the "new Soviet men." Usually engineers by training, they are the most highly paid people in the country, next to the intellectuals and top scientists. One of them said to me, "Profit is indispensable to production," and then added proudly—"I make a great deal of money."

They are all members of the Communist party and they take it for granted that "the party is the directing and guiding force of the national economy and its decisions are mandatory." Yet they seem to have little interest in ideology and politics. Their job is production and their interests are technical. Essentially practical and realistic, this managerial class has wrought the miracle of Soviet economic development.

Their approval of Khrushchev's reforms was uniform. But in Russia everyone approves of everything until it is suddenly changed, and then they vigorously denounce what yesterday they vigorously approved. Yet there can be no doubt of the improvement and they claim an 11 per cent increase in the first half of 1958 over 1957.

But there are bugs still to be ironed out. "Sectionalism" has been the biggest problem. The government works out production plans for all the regions and the interrelations between the regions. At first the new regional councils were more interested in overfulfilling their own goals (there is a bonus for overfulfillment) than helping other regions fulfill theirs. Mr. Stepanov illustrated.

"The Sverdlovsk region is rich in timber. Ukraine and Uzbekistan need timber. But some Sverdlovsk officials want all the local timber for local uses. As the old Russian proverb goes, 'Your own shirt is closer to your body,' and to want to look after yourself first is only natural. But the regional councils must keep the interests of the state as a whole constantly in mind."

The new Soviet seven-year plan of industrial development sets some spectacular objectives of productivity. The old goals of 1972 will almost be reached by 1965 in steel, iron ore, cement, woolen goods, shoes, etc. Such explosive growth must foresee even better results from Khrushchev's reorganization and decentralization. And it also looks as though the hard-working Russians were in for a lot more hard work—to catch up with America.

CHAPTER VII

The Way People Live

IN BARELY a generation Russia has been transformed from a backward agrarian country into the second industrial power in the world. But at what price? To what extent has the surge of economic strength benefited the Russian people? What of their working conditions now? What has this rapid industrialization of a big backward country cost in terms of liberties and living standards? Has this formidable growth been squeezed out of the lives, hides and souls of the people, as we so often say?

The Moscow planners remain committed to the priority of capital goods rather than consumer goods. But the consumer—that forgotten man of Stalin's Russia—has lately been receiving more attention. The attempt now being made to rule without terror is one reason. And it is now becoming apparent that "the party" is no longer the only force in Soviet society; a public opinion is emerging among the masses, and the workers' revolts in the satellites were not overlooked in Moscow.

Another reason for concern for the consumer pertains to foreign policy: The all-out production "war" that Khrushchev has declared against us is a contest in the field of living standards as well as basic industry. He wants to persuade the peoples of the newly developing countries—and not simply by paper propaganda—that the Soviet way really is a short cut not just to national power but to material abundance.

Foreign observers all testify that a slow improvement of living standards has been taking place, or more accurately an easing of the extreme austerity which has been the lot of the ordinary Russians for many years. But by our standards, or even those of western Europe, life in Russia is still drab and hard. Ordinary people are still preoccupied with satisfying the basic needs for food, clothing and shelter. The hunger for goods of all kinds is intense, and the queues of stolid, patient women waiting for stores to open is still commonplace. For the most part the food isn't very good, but there appears to be plenty for all. Of consumer goods, clothing, furniture and the like, there is, however, an acute shortage. The Russian people are not unhappy, but they want better living conditions, and little by little they are getting them. It is, I think, a mistake to measure their state of well-being against ours. They don't know what we have. But they do know and are constantly reminded of what they did not have before the revolution.

While bread is very cheap, most foods seemed expensive. Rents are low (about 5 per cent or less of the average Russian's wage), but most manufactured goods are high. Automobiles, for example, are purposely priced at almost prohibitive levels. Coming from America the first thing you notice is that there are trucks but almost no automobiles on the streets, and thousands of people on the sidewalks. (Vehicles and pedestrians have a high degree of disdain for each other, and either to walk or ride is perilous.)

A two-and-one-half-ton truck (for sale only to official organizations) is priced lower than the smallest passenger car. The truck's price is 22,000 rubles, or $2,200 at the tourist rate of exchange of ten rubles to the dollar, while the small four-cylinder "Muscovite" sells for 25,000, and the larger and nicer "Volga," which I saw on the assembly lines of the big auto plant in Gorky, costs 40,000 rubles. And even if a Russian is able to pay 25,000 rubles for a "Muscovite" he may have to wait two or three years to get one.

Education is free as far as you can go. So is medical service. Bookstalls are literally everywhere and prices, like the quality, are low. The Russian appetite for the printed word is without equal. Everyone who can read *does*, and in every spare moment. But the inflow of ideas is carefully policed. Foreign broadcasts are often jammed, foreign newspapers excluded and books and authors carefully selected, as the shocking case of Boris Pasternak has recently reminded us. Books are published in far greater numbers than in this country, and the authors of foreign works are either not compensated at all or only by some mysterious caprice of the government publishing houses. Yet while practicing this shameless piracy they denounce the exploitation of labor by the Western "capitalists."

But clothing is very expensive and drab. A man's suit

of poor quality may cost 1,500 rubles. The classic Russian tunic, black boots and military-style cap have all but vanished since I was there last. The modern Soviet man is hatless and long-haired; he wears a shapeless double-breasted suit with bell-bottom trousers and no necktie. The price range of nylons is from 13 to 43 rubles a pair, which means for the average wage earner working half a day to a day and a half for a pair of stockings. In the main department store of a remote provincial city, we found that unattractive wool suits for women cost from 800 to 1,200 rubles, blouses from 77 to 200 and very simple rayon dresses from 116 to 144.

No wonder many people answered "clothing" when we asked them how they would spend a wage increase. Others said "furniture," where quality and prices, as well as supply, are even worse. But they weren't all so practical; our airplane hostess one day, a pretty Kazakh girl, said, "Oh, powder, lipstick and things like that," for cosmetics also are rare.

The children, on the other hand, are usually well dressed, well fed, well mannered and alert. By day their parents, walking briskly the way Americans do, or standing patiently in queues, usually look serious and often weary. But at night and on holidays in the parks of "Rest and Culture" and at theaters and games they seem cheerful and content.

(And, speaking of queues, they say that if three Muscovites met on a desert island they would form a queue. The line waiting to see the tomb of Lenin and Stalin in

Red Square is blocks long every day. There blond peasants from the Baltic join Cossacks from the Don, dark Uzbeks in embroidered caps, Kazakhs in their tall felt hats and vacationers from all over the vast Soviet Union. To this shrine of Communism also comes an incessant procession of Indians, Chinese, Indonesians—delegations of Communists from all over the world—and American tourists.)

In Russia there are no private shops as in Poland, and there is little to buy of interest to foreign visitors, who always notice that there is no advertising and no salesmanship. The women at the counters don't care whether you buy or not.

A walk through GUM, the big department store on Red Square, or a Soviet style show is standard for tourists. All day long, endless lines of people stroll slowly past the rows of little booths. Most seem to be window-shopping. Suddenly traffic stops. A crowd of shoppers is overflowing a booth. They are orderly but determined to buy a winter coat or a pair of children's shoes which the state has that day made available. Whatever it was, to us it would not seem worth waiting for, let alone at twice our price.

The cities of Russia are tidy and clean nowadays, the subways famous and foolishly magnificent, the plumbing terrible and the new construction going up everywhere apparently poor and hurried. Shop windows hardly exist, except in Moscow and those are bad. Boulevards are spacious and handsome, tree-lined, sometimes improved with fine parks in the center, and always flanked for miles with huge, somber, functional apartment buildings. The Stalinist "wedding cake" skyscrapers are happily a thing of the past, but new public buildings, hotels and the like, are often overdecorated with ponderous chandeliers, velvet drapes, heavy rugs, gilt, glass and stone, in socialist imitation of prerevolutionary bourgeois grandeur. Parks and squares are numerous and fine, billboards (and comics!) almost non-existent, and appalling combative statues, mostly of Lenin and Stalin, are everywhere. Trotsky, of course, is never seen or mentioned.

Old Russia was built of wood, but houses of the past are still to be found behind the big new façades of brick and plaster. And the fine palaces of the old nobility are now mostly government offices.

When I was in Russia thirty-two years ago the housing shortage in the cities was acute. It still is. When my sons spent the evening with a young Russian they had to walk through his parents' room to reach the one other room where the younger members of the family lived. And these people were luckier than many families who have to share a tiny apartment, taking their turns at the kitchen and bath.

A young woman told us her dearest wish. "I think I speak for everyone in Russia when I say 'a home of my own.' "

In every city the "mayor" told me that housing was his biggest problem. Right now Khrushchev's government is making a big push to "liquidate the housing shortage" in eleven years. This means providing everyone with the officially accepted "norm" of 9 square meters of dwelling space, or a little less than 100 square feet. Miles of monstrous and monotonous apartment buildings are under construction in every Soviet city. And the government and factories also encourage individuals to build cottages and apartments for themselves by loans and leaves with pay.

I can't tell you how or even where Premier Khrushchev and the top brass, the members of the Politburo, live, for that is still a closely guarded secret and you are never invited to an official's house. But I have a good idea, and they live very well indeed. Some other people, too, have quite adequate homes, and perhaps even a *dacha* or summer cottage in the country. For equality in such matters is not part of "socialism" any longer, and the revolutionary idea of "to each according to his need" has vanished without a trace, like so much of classic Communism. If the average urban worker earns about 800 rubles a month, the manager of a good-sized factory may draw down ten or fifteen times that amount in salary and bonuses, and enjoy such extras as a car and chauffeur.

But it should also be reported that the highest paid groups in Soviet Russia are the senior professors and scientists, the thinkers and artists. The Soviets do a better job than we do when it comes to respect and recognition of the creative responsibility for the continuity of their civilization.

Unemployment is practically non-existent, and changing jobs is no longer next to impossible, as in Stalin's
time. If a workman's wages are low according to our
standards, his other benefits are considerable, including
free medical examinations and hospitalization, and free
or cheap vacations with pay at government sanatoria or
rest homes for many, cheap and very good theaters, evening education and factory recreation clubs.

While I was there last summer, a new decree urged
the trade unions to look after the welfare interests of the
workers more vigorously as well as promote efficiency
and productivity. I heard that labor is participating in
management more and more since Khrushchev took control of industry away from the ministries in Moscow and
transferred it to regional economic councils. Production
plans for this year, in some factories at least, were dis-
cussed in advance in each shop. The "plant fund" or
profit of a factory is now used in agreement with the
trade union. The central committee of the regional
Soviet now fixes the ranges for executive salaries, and the
management sets salaries within those ranges. The same
is generally true of wage rates, but the trade union has a
say in the matter.

And the director of the great Uralmash factory at
Sverdlovsk in the Urals told me—at a sumptuous lunch
in his executive offices—that while he believed in the
principle of one-man management, he could not fire a
workman without "co-ordinating" with the union com-

mittee. But "co-ordinating" seemed to mean informing rather than getting consent.

The chairman of the trade union committee was sitting on my other side, and his vigorous approval of all the manager said fortified my impression that Soviet industrialists have no organized labor problem. Perhaps I should have said fortified my impression that trade unions are company affairs and that free trade unions as we understand them don't yet exist in the U.S.S.R.

"What about strikes?" I asked. "What about the Taft-Hartley Law?" they shot back, and one of them added, "If you repeal that law, American workers will be happy and won't strike any more!" When I explained that even Taft-Hartley does not deprive our workers of the right to strike, my very genial Soviet hosts replied that their workers have a "feeling of ownership," and besides, "lack reasons for striking." True, they went on, "differences of opinion" arise from time to time, but these were always adjusted amicably, and the trade union committee if necessary "explains to the workers why they were not right in raising this or that question." (If that weren't a quotation I would add an exclamation point!)

We have heard much about slave labor in Russia. Perhaps some camps still exist, probably in the far north. But the Stalin terror, the knock on the door at midnight, is over now.

Roman Rudenko, the Procurator General (Attorney General), said the secret police had been put "in their place," and that conviction now could only be by a court.

He talked freely about the many innocent "victims" of the late Stalin period and placed the blame on the police chief, Beria, now executed, rather than Stalin. As to how many had since been rehabilitated—"that's an internal affair." And the number of prisons or camps still remaining? "That's the business of the M.V.D." But everyone testifies that the fear of Stalin's time no longer exists.

What the contribution of forced labor has been to Russian industrialization I don't know, but the confiscation or "postponement" of 250,000,000,000 rubles of government bonds a couple of years ago was a major and involuntary capital contribution. Purchase of these bonds was compulsory. Yet the "postponement" of principal and interest for twenty years has caused surprisingly little protest, probably because the workers were so thankful when the government at the same time ended the compulsory savings system.

Interesting to me as a lawyer was Rudenko's information that there are only about sixteen thousand practicing lawyers in the Soviet Union as against our two hundred thousand. A new criminal code will soon be issued and there is talk of a genuine rule of law in the U.S.S.R. where the courts have been a mechanism of party control in the past. At a "People's Court" one day I listened to the case of a man who had been discharged because he returned late from his vacation. His defense was that he had been hurt. How? Bitten by a cobra while snake hunting. The judgment? Entitled to his job—he was a taxidermist.

There is, in short, a big discrepancy between the booming industrialization of Russia and the snail's pace of the people's living standards. The plants and mines and power stations—all the apparatus of a modern industrial civilization—are being installed and multiplied, but so far only a trickle of benefits has reached the mass of workers and peasants. To Russians themselves, from the men in the Kremlin to the men on the street, this is no secret. All over the country you see a slogan that reads: "Communism is the bright tomorrow of all mankind." But I suspect that a vast number of ordinary people in Russia are weary of being told about a "bright tomorrow" as they live through an endless succession of pretty dreary todays.

At all events, they have a tremendous appetite for recreation at the parks, for athletic contests, concerts, the ballet, the theater, the opera and the circus—though even here the propaganda themes are usually worked in. Tickets are cheap, the performing arts superb and performances usually packed with absorbed and discriminating audiences. And the best seats are always reserved, somehow, for visitors from abroad. The way the Soviet encourages and entertains visitors, especially from Asia, the Middle East and Africa, is something we should not overlook.

Night life is meager. But in the big centers, restaurants with dance orchestras are popular with those who can afford it. As everywhere in Europe, soccer football is the national sport. We went to a spirited game one evening in the big new stadium in Moscow which holds 110,000. It was filled with an enthusiastic, good-natured crowd, whose cheers or boos (they whistle to express approval) for the league-leading "Spartacus" (the trade union team) or "Torpedo" (the team of the Moscow Auto Works) sounded very much like home. During the intermission daredevil motorcycle races kept us as breathless as the Russians.

The health services in Russia have performed a miracle. Three-quarters of all Soviet doctors are women, and so is the very competent woman who was Minister of Health when I was there, Maria Kovrigina. She told me their achievements are a national pride, and pride is essential to the health of a nation.

They claim that the average life expectancy now is sixty-seven years, compared with thirty-two before the revolution. Even if the expectancy is lower, the progress is certainly something to be proud of. Students can enter the seventy-nine medical schools after high school, and Madame Kovrigina says they have more doctors per capita than we have. There, as here, the chief killers are heart disease and cancer. They are great believers in preventive medicine, and 20,000,000 persons over thirty-five are examined annually for cancer. They also have great faith in psychological influences on health and annually take hundreds of thousands of workers from their normal dreary surroundings to the many sanitaria along the Black Sea coast for refreshment and a change of scene.

Madame Kovrigina claims that the incidence of mental trouble is lower in the U.S.S.R. than elsewhere because the Russians have a simple, single purpose and a common aim—to build up the Soviet Union. But she also admitted that alcoholism is a problem in the Soviet Union too.

During my previous visit to Russia the anti-religious campaign was at its height. Today you no longer see the slogan of those times: "Religion is the opiate of the people." Since church and state reached an agreement in the thirties, some churches have been reopened, about as many as the congregations can support, a Russian Orthodox bishop told me. Some have been repaired and reopened as museums and historical monuments.

But the educational system still emphasizes atheism and church attendance is forbidden to party members. Yet I saw lots of babies being baptized; insurance perhaps. And after visiting Orthodox churches in several cities, as well as the Baptist church and synagogue in Moscow and the principal mosque in Tashkent, it is clear to me that organized religion is still vigorous. Indeed, we were told that church attendance is on the increase by the charming and hospitable priests who entertained us royally at the great Troitsa monastery of Zagorsk—the tomb of St. Sergius and "the holiest place in Russia."

One Sunday I was asked to speak to the congregation —two thousand and mostly standing—squeezed into the

Baptist church, the only Protestant church in Moscow. Three times each Sunday the church is jammed, mostly with older women in white *babushkas*, as in the Orthodox churches. The mixed choir was lovely, and it was a moving experience to talk to that devout congregation who couldn't understand a word and waited raptly for the translation of the message I tried to bring them from the free world. When I finished they waved white handkerchiefs and sang in Russian "God be with you till we meet again."

There are said to be 500,000 Jews in Moscow but there is only one synagogue. In the other cities our guides somehow could never find the synagogue at all. Under the Czars the persecuted Jews were permitted to emigrate. Today many would doubtless like to go to Israel but they are not permitted to. If Jews were permitted to leave, non-Jews might start wondering about life beyond the Curtain.

The question is what will be done about living conditions and when. The new economic development plan says the long period of forced austerity is about over, that a better life is at hand for the poor and patient Russians. The promises are sensational: in a few years per acre farm production will exceed present U.S. averages, real income will increase 40 per cent, per capita production will overtake ours, and the Russians will have the highest living standard and shortest working hours in the world. And the plan also stresses the need for peace if it is to be completed on schedule.

If it comes to pass as promised, will the example of Soviet success attract the poor neutral nations to the Communist bloc in hopes of doing the same? And if Russia reaps the benefits of industrialization can fear and despotism survive for long in an affluent society?

CHAPTER VIII

The Siberian Colonists

ONE of the memorable sights you see if the Russians let you travel as far east as Sverdlovsk in the Urals is a white stone shaft in a birch and pine forest by the side of a winding road about thirty miles east of town. Two words are carved on it side by side: "Europe" and "Asia." And of course you have your picture taken with one foot in Europe and the other in Asia.

To the east, across the largest plain in the world to the highlands beyond and on to the Pacific, stretches the one-third of Asia called Siberia—a territory bigger than the whole U.S.A. and thrice the size of western Europe. The Russians started colonizing it at the end of the sixteenth century, when the Cossack Yermak and his followers crossed the Urals. They are still colonizing it, and today Nikita Khrushchev is striving to finish up the job that Yermak started. "Go east, young man," is his slogan.

I wanted to go there particularly because Siberia, together with the enormous arid Kazakh Republic on the south, is the U.S.S.R.'s new frontier. In his public report to the 20th Soviet Party Congress (which is not so well known abroad as the "secret" one denouncing Stalin), Khrushchev called for the "mobilization of the immense natural resources of the eastern regions," and forecast that in ten years Siberia will become an industrial arsenal, producing tremendous quantities of steel, iron, coal and electric power.

How great those resources are was suggested at my meeting with the Academy of Science in Novosibirsk, the big city of western Siberia. Siberia, they said, possesses 80 per cent of all the U.S.S.R.'s coal deposits, 75 per cent of the timber, 60 per cent of the hydroelectric power resources and over half of the iron ore, non-ferrous metals and copper. Already it produces 70,000,000 tons of coal yearly (more than France) in the great Kuznetsk Basin. As for Kazakhstan, its mineral wealth is so varied that the members of its Academy of Science summed it up by saying they had found "all the elements of the Mendelyev system."

They also said, in answer to my question, that Malenkov, Khrushchev's predecessor, was living at the remotest end of Kazakhstan. I couldn't resist the temptation to add that as defeated head of the "opposition" in the United States I was at liberty to say what I pleased and go where I pleased—including the Soviet Union. My host quickly answered, "Why don't you invite Malenkov to the U.S.?" Maybe it would be a good idea!

Agriculture has been the Soviet's biggest failure, and Mr. Khrushchev's bold solution is to make these empty eastern regions the main granary of the U.S.S.R. He has apparently succeeded with his daring plan to reorganize industry. But success is less predictable for his plan to plow up huge areas of virgin soil in south Siberia and Kazakhstan.

Since 1954, when the "new lands" program was started,

they say that about 90,000,000 new acres have become productive. By raising more bread grains on the new lands Khrushchev hopes to free land in the warm fertile southwest—the Ukraine and Caucasus—for what he regards as "queen of the fields," corn. With more corn he can fatten more livestock and hurry the day when Russia can "catch up with America in meat, butter and eggs," a sign we saw at every farm.

Initially some 300,000 young people were coaxed or pressured to go out as "volunteers" to till the virgin lands. In 1956 about 2,000,000—mostly students—were sent out for the summer to help with the harvest. But that experiment with "soft hands" from the city harvested mostly blisters and sunburn.

I suspect the men in the Kremlin have one eye anxiously cocked at the exploding population of Siberia's neighbor, "fraternal" Communist China, which is another good reason for settling these immense empty spaces. A measure of the desire to populate Siberia is the recent decision of the Young Communist League to send out a million youths as settlers in the coming few years.

In Kazakhstan we visited a kolkhoz, a collective farm at the foot of the snow-capped Tien Shan Mountains on the border of China. On a hundred thousand acres of farm and pasture land 1,680 families lived, of twenty-one nationalities. The 2,600 able-bodied workers raised everything from grain to grapes in commercial quantities. The livestock included cattle, horses, pigs, poultry, bees, silver foxes, 40,000 sheep and 180 camels! (Incidentally, thirty-five people were assigned to look after the 1,500 "Russian white" pigs, which illustrates the labor waste all over Russia.)

On these farms each family has an acre or so around its house for itself—the amount varies—and can sell any surplus produce in the free market in town. A farmer's earnings are computed in workday units and paid in cash and produce. The average income seems to be somewhat lower than a city worker's, but there is a high degree of self-sufficiency and a farmer's living costs must be much lower. I even saw an old-fashioned spinning wheel in use in a peasant's house on one of these farms.

This farm boasted a large "club" with an auditorium seating five hundred for recreation and political "education." Just as in the city factories, the babies and small children were kept in very good nurseries and kindergartens while their mothers were at work on the farm. Walking through a sugar beet field we stopped to talk with a "work brigade," mostly women. When the manager said they worked ten hours a day, "but in the winter they have nothing to do," one of them behind me muttered, "We work." And I'll bet they do!

Prices are now fixed in advance on all collective production. This farm had just purchased from the Machine Tractor Station the machinery it formerly rented. The rental was payable on a complicated basis in cash, grain and operators' wages. With prices certain and higher and no more machine rentals to pay, the farm manager was happy. And, best of all, he said the changes had reduced "the bookkeeping and the bureaucrats." But I couldn't get a comprehensible estimate of the farm's net earnings —perhaps because he was an ex-bookkeeper in a government bureau.

This delightful man, who wore the red star of a "hero of Soviet labor" on his white tunic, explained that he knew nothing of farming until he was assigned the big job of managing this farm. And when he proudly told me that his son teaches history he added, with a wry grin, "But if the government wants him to be a farmer, he'll be a farmer too!"

Stalin would never agree to liquidate the Machine Tractor Stations by selling the machinery to the farmers. He predicted it would undermine the Soviet system. But Khrushchev has done it. And putting the machinery in the hands of those who have the best incentive for using it efficiently is certainly popular and should pay dividends.

But what does Siberia look like? If you go there at the season I did, it doesn't at all square with your image of bleak frozen wastes. My first glimpse was on a warm July day after landing in an open field—an island in a sea of green grain—near the small south Siberian town of Rubtsovsk, one of the centers of the new lands program. A deputation of genial sunburned dignitaries met us. One short, bowlegged, leathery man was introduced as the director of the Yegorievsky state farm. Had he said "Howdy, pardner" instead of "*Zdravstvuite*" (that impossible Russian word for "hello"), I don't think I'd have been surprised.

At a respectful distance was a large crowd of curious townsfolk. And we were never without a crowd of friendly smiling people from that time on.

Coming from the ancient oriental atmosphere of Central Asia to Rubtsovsk that day was like coming from the Near East to our own Great Plains, as they used to be many years ago. Our cars raised clouds of dust on the dirt road and skirted around the mudholes through fenceless oceans of wheat and oats billowing out endlessly under a clear blue sky. Off on the flat, treeless horizon a freight train chugged slowly along, black smoke trailing from the old steam locomotive. The wail of the distant whistle reminded me of my boyhood on the prairies of the Middle West, and it was hard to believe that it was the Turk-Sib railroad and not the Illinois Central. We drove into town past straggling log houses, a huge grain elevator, a war-built tractor plant and finally into the imposing new main square. At the Rubtsovsk hotel another large crowd of curious Siberians was awaiting us.

In this cold climate greenery is much esteemed and my hotel room was largely occupied by an enormous bush that looked like hibiscus. And in the bookshelves were more surprises—Dickens, Jack London, Stevenson, Galsworthy, O. Henry, Thackeray, Steinbeck and Sinclair Lewis.

We drove forty miles into the country to see the Yegorievsky state farm, accompanied by the personable vice-chairman of the provincial soviet, Vasily Gordeev.

As we careened along I thought of Illinois before the hard roads, and then we got stuck in the mud. The wheat, barley and oats reminded me of home too. The rainfall had been exceptional this year and their best harvest was expected.

We talked with Gordeev about Soviet-American competition, and one memory of this trip I will always retain was the disappointment on his genial, handsome face when I said we were not competing on farm production. And then his dejection turned to incredulity when I said that in the U.S. we had too much food and fiber. But when I added we even paid farmers not to produce he gave me the sly, amused wink of a politician not unfamiliar with gullible audiences.

The Yegorievsky farm had over 50,000 acres and a work force of 650. Like most of the "new lands" farms, it was a sovkhoz, a state farm, rather than a kolkhoz, or collective. The latter are theoretically run on a co-operative basis, but a sovkhoz is a state enterprise like a factory, and its farmers work for wages like factory workers. A regular field hand at the Yegorievsky "grain factory" receives 600 to 800 rubles a month, or $60 to $80 at the tourist rate of exchange.

This year, the manager told me, they were not going to count on students from the distant cities at harvest time. And I learned that many of the young "volunteers" sent east in the great resettlement campaign (100,000 of them were sent to this province) have since returned. But most of those who marry seem to be willing to settle down in Siberia.

Wheat is the main crop, and the brisk little manager expected a yield of better than thirty bushels an acre, as against twenty-eight last year. At another big farm we visited the following day—a kolkhoz this time—they said their yield last year was twenty-four bushels to the acre.

The grain is stored on the ground or in long, low, mud-brick sheds, and much of the machinery—including huge self-propelled combines—has no shelter at all. I never saw a silo in Russia, and the silage, mostly green corn, is stored in ditches.

But I did see dwarfed apple and cherry trees bred to live *under* the Siberian snows. And in the middle of an orchard we sat down at long wooden tables to eat piles of the first raspberries grown out of doors in Siberia, where the first frost comes in late August and the reliable growing season is only about one hundred days.

Typical horse-drawn Russian carts are far more numerous than automobiles along the dirt roads where cattle and chickens feed at will. And life in the isolated remote farm communities must be much as it was on our frontier a century ago. But there is a difference—tractors and schools; and social life centers not around a church, but around a party clubhouse ornamented with oversize statues of Lenin and Stalin and propaganda signs.

Some Western observers have predicted that Khrushchev is plowing up a gigantic future dust bowl on these marginal or semimarginal lands in the east. Even in southern Siberia the rainfall is uncertain. When a U.S. farm delegation visited Rubtsovsk in 1955—a dry year—

they saw dust clouds up to three thousand feet. But this year is a good one, and the crops were certainly impressive. As to ultimate success or failure, it is too soon to write it off as a certain failure. And certainly it is also too soon to conclude that Khrushchev has solved his farm problems.

From Rubtsovsk we flew north to Novosibirsk, once a labor camp where the Trans-Siberian crosses the Ob River, and now the "Siberian Chicago." I think it pleased the mayor when I gave him greetings from my friend Richard Daley, the mayor of a more familiar Chicago. Here, too, our first impressions were strangely un-Siberian. But a little of old Siberia survives in the sturdy blue-shuttered log houses on Novosibirsk's cobbled side streets.

Mr. Khrushchev is not only mobilizing young people to settle and cultivate the new frontier, but also top scientists to chart the development of Siberia. And my talk concluded with a question from Academician H. A. Thinakal, a great mining engineer and a humorous elderly man, who asked if I was disappointed not to find any bears in Siberia. I told him I was no more disappointed than he would be not to find Indians in Indiana. "Long ago," he said, "I spent some time in the United States and returned convinced that if you would dress Americans and Russians alike you could not tell them apart." And I agreed.

CHAPTER IX

Education the Soviet Way

SOVIET education became an object of respectful curiosity for many Americans when the first Soviet sputnik jolted us out of our national complacency.

What we discovered was that education is a mighty serious business in the U.S.S.R., that learning is highly valued, that scholarship commands the highest salaries, that the hunger for knowledge is great and that reading and self-education are the universal pastime of Russians.

And we also discovered that the Soviet Union had made astonishing progress. Not only had this vast backward country, in which only half the people speak Russian as their native tongue, become almost totally literate in barely a generation, but it had overtaken or surpassed the rest of the world in the physical sciences.

And so I was surprised to learn in Russia that the Soviet leaders are dissatisfied with their educational system, and plan to give it a radical overhauling. While here in the United States we are debating whether Johnny gets enough solid intellectual work, in Russia they are concerned whether Ivan is being prepared for life and work in the Soviet Union or just for the university.

Education, like most everything else in Russia, is controlled by the government and the Communist party.

The Ministry of Education in Moscow controls the elementary and secondary schools, and the Ministry of Higher Education the general institutions of higher learning.

In each of the Republics there is an identical structure of nurseries, kindergartens, ten-year schools, technical schools and universities. The government research organization is the great Academy of Science in Moscow, and it has a branch in each Republic. It is these top Academicians who get the big salaries, the big automobiles and the country homes, which make them the most favored people in Russia. And the budgets of these Academies of Science exceed by many times the budgets for the teaching institutions such as the universities.

Since Stalin's death the scientists have been enlisted to help plan the nation's development. Some thirty commissions of scientists and government officials have worked out the economic plans for 1959-65. They decide what resources are to be developed, what industries enlarged, how many engineers, doctors, teachers, researchers, linguists, etc., will be needed and where. And then it is up to the Education Ministries to fill the planners' prescriptions through the system of efficient academic factories.

Evgeni Afanasenko, the personable young Minister of Education in Moscow, frankly and firmly stated the basic difference between our systems: "Here *we* decide what they are to learn." The Ministries choose the textbooks and determine the curriculum. American experts say that standards of academic and research work are high, probably generally higher than ours, because no "local" interference is permitted.

Service to the state, in short, is the objective of the entire intellectual and educational apparatus of the Soviet Union. It is in sharp contrast to our conviction that the fullest, freest development of each individual's potential will yield the best service to his fellow man.

The control and direction of education and training begins at the cradle, in collective day nurseries, followed by kindergartens, where in group work and play children learn the collectivist way of life and that the party and the state are all-wise, all-good, all-powerful. I was impressed each time by the obvious competence and devotion of the personnel, and by the equipment and efficiency of these institutions. And, as a grandfather, I also observed that Russian babies seldom cry, and the very young children are quiet and well behaved.

The Russians believe that six is too young to begin formal education, and their schools commence at seven. Schooling is obligatory for only seven years in the country and ten years in the city, although Mr. Khrushchev has lately revealed that 20 per cent of the Soviet children do not complete even the seven-year program.

While intellectual and ideological development is being attended to in the schoolroom, the children's leisure is not neglected. From seven to twenty-six, Soviet young people are expected to join a series of youth organizations —the Little Octobrists, the Young Pioneers, finally the

Young Communist League—which provide carefully balanced programs of athletic activities, the arts, vocational training and ideological indoctrination. And if you are a Young Pioneer you'd better be careful about going to church with grandma!

We visited a better-than-average "Palace of Young Pioneers" in Sverdlovsk in the Urals. It was housed in a huge old mansion, once owned by a mining magnate. There school children occupy leisure hours with sports, the arts and sciences, photography, handicrafts and building models of everything from coal mines to atomic energy plants. In the surrounding park we saw a children's experimental garden plot and orchard, and a first-rate puppet theater where children were performing their own plays.

And their own newspaper, *Pioneer Pravda,* was telling the ten- to fifteen-year-olds exactly what the adult *Pravda* was telling their elders: about the "American aggression" against Lebanon. A front-page editorial entitled "Stop The Warmongers!" informed the Young Pioneers that the "capitalists" were hanging on to the Middle East "the way a maddened beast holds on to its prey."

At the end of the compulsory schooling period those who "haven't proved themselves" go to work. The better qualified ones (or those better situated in society) may go on to one of the 3,500 "technicums" for training as technical specialists. I visited a typical technicum in Siberia. Attached to a big machine-building plant, it trains youngsters aged fifteen and up in machine building. Its eight hundred students, taught by a staff of thirty teachers and aided by specialists from the factory, receive some general education in history and the Russian language along with technical training during the first year and a half. But the rest of the five-year curriculum is strictly technical, and 30 per cent of the time is devoted to production practice in the factory.

Evidently "comradely competition" to go on to higher education is pretty fierce among secondary school students. On completion of a full ten years of schooling the lucky ones selected by competitive testing may enter one of 700-odd specialized institutions or thirty-five universities. I say "lucky" because last year over 700,000 ten-year-school graduates were not admitted to higher education. Only 450,000 freshmen are admitted each year, half of whom study in the day session and half at night. The struggle intensifies up the ladder. I was told, for example, by Madame Kovrigina, at that time the Soviet Minister of Health, that there are over fifteen applications per vacancy in the medical schools in Moscow and eight to ten elsewhere in the country.

The poor boy struggling for an education is unknown. More than 80 per cent of the college students receive stipends from the state of 400 to 600 rubles per month, according to their ability. And the favored position in Soviet society of the intellectual also insures that after graduation the best students stay in education or research. There is no rush to industry, as in this country, because the salaries in education and research are higher than industry is permitted to pay.

Most faculty members do not belong to the Communist party. And I got the impression that student interest in Communist ideology and in the required indoctrination courses is languid at best. If true, that would be quite a change from the excitement of the young people about Marxism and the world revolution when I was in Russia in 1926. Now they are interested in efficiency, production, a better life and more contact with the outside world.

I was also struck by the large role women play in education. A third of the university faculties and half of the students are said to be women. In the medical schools Madame Kovrigina told me two-thirds of the students were women. And she freely expressed her misgivings about women doctors, because their first interest was usually marriage and a family and not the profession. But certainly the Soviet use of womanpower, from the heaviest manual labor to the most qualitative scholarship and research, is something to think about in the struggle between our two systems.

But I began by saying that the Soviets were overhauling their educational system. From what Minister Afanasenko and other officials told me, I gather the trouble is that there are too many applicants for higher education, and not enough labor, especially during the next few years when the age groups born in the baby-lean war years enter the economy. Evidently too many young people in the "workers' state" prefer the white-collar class, the "intelligentsia" of professional people, specialists and administrators. And the planners' solution is to make the school system job-oriented rather than college-oriented.

Mr. Afanasenko did not put it to me in just this way. The Soviet Union, he said, now finds itself in a position to realize the "ancient idea" of merging education and productive labor—an idea of the utopian socialists which was taken up by Marx and Lenin, and has now been espoused by Premier Khrushchev. To do this they propose to replace the present ten-year school system with a basic eight-year school which will give all Soviet children a "general polytechnical education" and a thorough grounding in the fundamentals of science. The pupils, he stressed, will be taught not only good work habits but also that "human life is unthinkable without labor." They will be prepared psychologically for a life of work.

After the eight-year period specialized high schools will admit the young people who have disclosed extraordinary promise. But the great majority will go from the eight-year school, at the age of sixteen, into industry and agriculture. Those who want to continue studying can do so on a part-time basis while working. And they may enter college later if they show real ability—and if the trade union or Young Communist League recommends them for higher education. The result, said Mr. Afanasenko, will be that Soviet youths will not grow up to be "idlers" or "white-handed ones."

The new system will be introduced in 1960. And it is a safe prediction that the competition for advanced education is going to get more intense in the Soviet Union, and with it the standards of technical proficiency will rise still higher.

One aspect of Soviet education I cannot leave unmentioned is languages. The older academics are not much better than we Americans at language. But the young people are getting five years of foreign language and four more at the university level. The choice of half is English; then German and French. And it won't be long before the Russians will have a great advantage in every exchange—cultural, political and propaganda.

Another formidable fact that must be added to the new enthusiasm and emphasis on qualitative achievement is the large Soviet expenditure for education. Some American experts estimate that the Russians value it at least twice as highly as we do; they spend twice the percentage of their national income that we spend of ours.

I mentioned earlier the City of Science which is being constructed in Siberia to accommodate fourteen scientific institutes, a university for five thousand students and a population of twenty-five thousand—all for the economic development of Siberia. There will be modern cottages for top scientists, small apartment houses for the others, garages, theaters, a sports stadium and all community facilities. It will be the Soviet Union's first suburban community development of the kind so familiar to us in America. It is characteristic of Soviet Russia that the first such residential development should make its appearance in the middle of Siberia—and for the purpose of education, research and economic development, which are certainly Russia's first priorities.

But with all of its strengths, its amazing achievements and bold plans, Russian education falls far short of what we want. The Soviets have a passion for black and white, for a single solution for every problem—the official solution. They do not understand choice. Hence the curriculum is rigid and does not encourage individual creative thinking and originality. Soviet education is a tool for the achievement of the state's purposes. It may be successful in preparing youth for a life of service to the Soviet state. But it would not prepare youth for our society, where the goal of education is the harmonious development of the individual in and for himself.

There was hope after Stalin for greater intellectual freedom, but the world recently suffered a stunning blow from the old iron fist of Soviet conformity. Boris Pasternak wrote: "What has for centuries raised man above the beast is not the cudgel but an inward music: the irresistible power of unarmed truth, the powerful attraction of its example."

And look what happened to him!

CHAPTER X

Is Coexistence Possible?
Some Disturbing—and Some Hopeful—Conclusions

NOT long ago Soviet Russia was lightly discounted in America as a serious competitor in atomic energy, industrial production, scientific development, education and political influence. More recently we have been told from high places that the Soviet system is shaky and that if we hold fast its own obvious ills will destroy it.

So I went to Russia to see for myself. In earlier chapters I have reported some of my impressions; now I should like to record a few of my conclusions.

The first is that we have been badly informed and are badly mistaken. The Soviet Union is a stable power system and is not on the brink of internal collapse. The reasonable hope is not that it will disintegrate but that it may evolve into something less aggressive and menacing to peace and human freedom.

The second is that Russia is not the largest question mark in America's future. It is number two. Our number one problem is China—and so is Russia's. But the lengthening shadow of China is another subject.

Our emotional reaction to the rise of Communism has

been to reject reality, aided and abetted of late by our political leaders. We were not prepared for sputnik or the Soviet economic challenge. But the illusion of our superiority in everything, together with the denial of unpleasant realities, is a bad basis for foreign policy. I hope we are fast approaching the end of this era of innocence and ignorance.

When I say the Soviet regime is stable I don't mean there is no internal dissension. I have no doubt there is bitter controversy over policy and sinister plotting for power in the Kremlin. One of the worst indictments of the Soviet system is that after forty years they have not worked out a means of transferring power without conspiracy, exile and violence.

What I mean by stability is that if life is austere and hard, at least it is getting better and there are no signs of rebellion. That does not mean that all Russians are devout Communists. Actually, only a fraction of the adults belong to the party. But if they are not the mass of indoctrinated zealots, the 200,000,000 enthusiastic Communists that some have portrayed, neither are they the mass of sullen, terrorized helots, seething with rebellion, that others have pictured. They seemed to me like most people—loyal, obedient and patriotic, proud of Russia as a great nation and of her achievements to which they contributed.

The industrial development, as I have said, has been spectacular. Even the chronic lag in farm production shows signs of responding to new remedies. While two-thirds of our output goes to the consumer, in Russia the consumer has had to do without and two-thirds has gone to industrial development, with a high priority for military strength and foreign aid and trade. The economic goal is to catch up with America in per capita production. And the new seven-year economic plan confidently predicts that the Soviet Union will pass us in total and per capita production and give the Russian people the world's highest living standards by 1970 or before.

The political goal is to displace the United States as the foremost world power, and, as it always has been, to make the whole world Communist. And the leaders confidently expect to do that too, although the timetable is elastic.

The jolly, agile and able boss, Nikita Khrushchev, talked earnestly about better Russian-American relations and agreed with me that non-interference with other states was a good place to start. But his interpretation seemed to be non-interference by everybody—except the U.S.S.R. And his testy talk about Hungary, Poland and Yugoslavia echoed the stresses and strains in the satellite empire where the peoples have long histories of freedom and independence and are ruled by uneasy minority Communist governments. Russia's satellites in Europe are a perpetual source of insecurity.

And I have no doubt that they will try to eliminate the dangerous free island of West Berlin in the heart of East Germany, because, as Hungary showed, they are resolved to keep their uneasy empire intact.

But internally the Soviet Union appears to be stable, strong, and getting stronger. Khrushchev's Russia is not static. However, for all the developments and changes in industry, agriculture and other fields there is no alteration of the totalitarian structure. And my guess is that Mr. Khrushchev has no intention of presiding over the dissolution of the Soviet dictatorship—not, as he vividly puts it, "until the shrimps whistle." Rather the purpose of these capital repairs on the dictatorship seems to be to modernize and adapt the administrative system to the needs of a dynamic, growing industrial economy, to make the country economically more productive, militarily more powerful, administratively more efficient, more modern in appearance, more normal in atmosphere —and thereby give the dictatorship a new lease on life and strengthen the one-party system.

The Soviet challenge is formidable, and it will be with us for a long time to come. I think they have given up trying to take over the advanced countries, like France and Italy, and the greatest danger is not in Europe but in Asia and Africa. Already Soviet technicians and salesmen have established economic beachheads in many poor countries struggling to develop, and without any military strings attached. The Soviet example of rapid and successful industrialization of an illiterate, backward country has a great attraction for the newly developing people who live like Russian peasants and are demanding a better life. And of course the irrelevance to them of the Soviet example, the brutality of the means and the heavy price in democratic values are not at first apparent.

Five years ago I wrote and have often repeated that Soviet economic growth was "a more important fact than the development of Soviet military power, and to many people in the underdeveloped countries it is the single most impressive fact about the Communist world." And a year ago I urged our government to give economic development equal priority with defense at the NATO meeting in Paris, because if sustained economic growth under democratic auspices fails, people will turn to the Soviet example.

I came away from the Soviet Union more convinced than ever that the battle of the future is economic and political and the major battleground is in Asia and Africa. They are trying to persuade the neutrals to secede from the capitalist system and will exploit to the fullest their enormous appeal as a backward and non-colonial country that has "made good."

There were other disturbing conclusions. Perhaps the single most disturbing thing about Soviet Russia is the ignorance of these friendly, warmhearted people about us.

"Why do you have two parties?" an intelligent ex-schoolteacher and district boss asked me. "Here we are not antagonistic; we all have the same goals; we all work for one another." I said something about the people having a choice of men and measures. "But here," he said, "the Communist party includes the best and knows what's best. So how could there be any question of choice?" It all seemed a little hopeless—especially while careening across the Siberian steppe from mudhole to mudhole.

They know little of our life and motives; most of them, I suspect, sincerely believe that we made the Iron Curtain and for some mysterious reason may attack them at any moment, as the incessant propaganda proclaims. How the ordinary people can continue to be so friendly, hospitable and admiring about America baffles me. Their instincts are good, and it is depressing that they can't know that ours are, too.

It is important, I believe, for us to make every possible effort to lessen their ignorance of our country and its democratic way of life. But likewise we need to study them hard and try by every means for better understanding and deeper appreciation of the conditions of life, attitudes, values and ideas, of the Russian people and their Communist masters. We need to know much more than we do about the mind of this 200,000,000-strong people, who are destined to play a very big part in history and with whom we must hope to live as peaceful neighbors on a shrunken planet. In short, we should do everything we can to increase contact and to encourage Russians to come here and Americans to go there.

Russia is only now emerging from a revolution that stretches far back of the Bolshevik Revolution. What individual freedom under law means is hard for people who have never had it to understand, but it is our most precious possession and we should be proud and eager to exhibit it; besides, it is the best hope for the future.

I wish all the Soviet bosses—the Ministers, the members of the party Presidium and even Mr. Khrushchev himself—could come to this country, because most of them seem to be imprisoned by their own propaganda and laboring under many delusions. Even if they are not deluded, but cynical and insincere, it is harder to be that way after you have come to know something of a country and a people.

My happiest conclusion is that the Russians don't want war any more than we do. The people, who suffered so horribly in the last war, don't want it for obvious reasons; the leaders because it would interrupt their great development program, and because they believe the manifest destiny of Sovietism is to inherit the earth from "decadent capitalism" anyway.

Khrushchev's phrase was "We will bury you." But he did not mean that they would kill us first. On the contrary, I concluded that they would use their arms cautiously, knowing from experience that any further expansion by force means war because we would intervene. I suspect they realize, too, that Stalin was the principal architect of NATO because he frightened us.

I wish I felt that our defensive bases in Europe, North Africa and the Middle East did not provide Khrushchev and Co. such a convenient peg for propaganda about America's offensive threat. But while it has been an article of Communist faith that dying capitalism would fight its way out, I also concluded that the Soviet leaders may no longer believe in the inevitability of war. The reasoning is that the Soviet system will be so strong the West won't dare to fight. Even if this vision of a supine, expiring capitalism seems psychotic to us, a change of heart about the inevitability of war would be significant and hopeful.

And there are other encouraging signs. One is the decline in fanaticism. Many of the younger rising Soviet leaders have been trained as engineers and economists and spend their careers in administration. In this new managerial elite, ideology gets more lip service than passion. They are not doctrinaire gamblers and revolutionaries trying to seize power, but realistic practical people trying to make the Soviet system work better. And I think they will be easier to deal with as they replace the older generation of combat Communists.

A related hope is that with economic improvement and better living conditions in Russia we will have more in common and the enmity of inferiority will diminish. With more self-confidence it is not unreasonable to expect that the areas of scientific, economic and political co-operation will broaden and reduce the divisions and tensions. As Russia becomes a modern, industrialized and rich society it will move along a path similar to that traversed by the other industrial societies of the West. It may not be the same path, but, like other nations, Russia, too, must evolve. And we know that in highly developed societies it is not so easy to fool, frighten and mislead the people.

Once Soviet policy and politics focus on economic

welfare and the Russian people have a taste of the mass consumer's age (even automobiles!) there will be no turning back from the welfare state and all that implies for Bolshevism as we have known it.

A wise Pole said to me last summer that the changes in Western capitalism and the changes in Soviet Communism are bringing us imperceptibly together in the center. The day is not far distant, he said, when only a few politicians on both sides who are chained to the old semantics will still be talking about two totally opposed worlds.

We laughed together about the prospect of capitalism subverting Communism, and Russian officials struggling with toll roads, suburbia, gas stations and the rest.

But all that is for the future—if not the birds.

Meanwhile the reality is the remorseless Soviet challenge which we have too long ignored and underestimated. They will use their greater flexibility to keep us off balance and on the defensive. They will continue to picture us as menacing and rigid to the Afro-Asian bystanders. They will make agreements only when it serves their purpose. Suspending nuclear tests with inspection is a hopeful possibility and would be the first break in the armaments deadlock. But I am less hopeful of Soviet agreement to larger measures of inspection of their territory because it would tend to convert their closed system into an open one and thus endanger the basis of Soviet control.

While I think the intensity of the Soviet system will

decline in time, I see little hope for early change. On the other hand, there is the constant danger that we will fall asleep again.

If we can't do much with Moscow, we can do a lot with ourselves. The free world must set its house in order and keep it in order, and not just sit around, bickering, postponing and waiting for total peace to break out. Moscow will be more likely to talk seriously if the Western alliance is vital and viable, the residual colonial problems being dealt with (while the reality of Soviet imperialism becomes more obvious), and above all the free world making a concerted effort to unite the advanced and retarded areas in common economic enterprises.

I think we must plug patiently away at stopping the arms race, with international supervision, and forego any lingering ideas of military superiority which will only accelerate the arms race. I think it would be most realistic and helpful if we recognized the principle of equality with the Soviet Union. And we should always be ready to talk with them at all levels, but with little hope of quick success. Time is of no importance to them, as it is of no importance to Orientals, and the hope is that little by little we can break away from the concept of each other as the enemy and reduce fear and distrust.

I have seen the Russians close up. They are tough, fearful and going places. But they are also very human and friendly. Their hopes and desires are for peace—and an apartment. The leaders are scornful of "capitalism," yet even Khrushchev wants to attain the American standard of living more than anything else. And we still have the supreme advantage of living under the system most people want if they can get it and afford it.

This should give us calm and final confidence.